A Warrior's JOURNEY

WITH A Compassionate Dragon!

ANA V. ARANGO AND
CHRISTOPHER C. COLE

outskirts
press

Outskirts Press, Inc.
http://www.outskirtspress.com

Paperback ISBN: 978-1-9772-4398-0
Hardback ISBN: 978-1-9772-4401-7

Outskirts Press and the "OP" logo are trademarks belonging to Outskirts Press, Inc.

PRINTED IN THE UNITED STATES OF AMERICA

Dedication

The spirit of Kannon's love and kindness has always lived in my heart and guided me protectively through my life's thoughts, decisions, adventures, and compassion for others. It is in the spirit of her love and kindness that I wish to dedicate this book to those who were there at my beginning and gave me multifaceted gifts of knowledge, awareness, and strengths. Ambitions and enthusiasm were passed to me from my Abuelo Pedro (a man who up to his last day on earth, at age 105, was planning a new business to open). Spirituality was lovingly presented to me by my Abuela Ana (a shaman and a revolutionist). My beloved father entrusted me with honesty (first by late-night readings of Pinocchio, later with Confucius readings and hours-long conversations and always by his impeccable example of being a man of honor). My treasured mother in moments of fearfulness contained within herself a grandeur of courage to face all obstacles. I am so grateful to have inherited her courage. Lastly, from my dear Aiki Dragon, who before my birth embraced me with his gentleness of joy and laughter, I have been regally bestowed with the far-reaching wings of adventure. My dear Aiki Dragon is real, powerful, and exists in and beyond our universe, where with his fierce and friendly healing, dragon energies have benevolently lived in my heart and soul manifesting readiness and determination for me to be a multidimensional adventurer. From all of their excellences, these wonderful, dynamic, and generous-natured guardians of wisdom and truths have created within me the beautiful, rhythmic energy of love needed to walk the peaceful, compassionate warrior's path.

Table of Contents

Introduction

Spirit of Dragon

Please let me introduce myself. My name is Aiki Dragon and I have been on earth for longer than the length of humankind. Although not everyone can see me, I am here and I am everywhere. One ageless soul who can see me is my dear Anita Aiki Dragon. I have always been with her, as one of her many guardians and protectors, and through the years she has learned to know me well. Dear Anita met me through what seemed to be a dream to her, but I was truly there in person (as her Abuela Ana looked on). How lovely it was to be with her as she became aware that she, too, was a part of the World of Dragons. My dear Anita and I have discussed many things, primarily of getting a book out for others to learn and be enlightened regarding the ways of the dragons, the simple truths of being, the creative powers of enthusiasm, perseverance, and self-trust, to have compassion for others, to never allow anyone to tell you no, the gift of friendships, the excellent health found in the preventions of Chinese medicine, self-reflection of spirituality, the loving strength of a beautiful goddess named Kannon, the healing powers of a Dragon Queen, the love and harmony of Aikido, and the timeless world of synchrodestiny, which unites souls with souls within the Universe. My dear Anita and my wishes are to share gratitude and love with you through dear Anita's life journeys so we may introduce to you the Universe's love, wisdom, wonderment, and truths and you, too, may join in the warrior's walk of peace, compassion, and empowerment.

Chapter 1

Aiki Dragon

Trust Self. Trust Universe. Trust Dragon.

Please let me explain about myself, dragons, and our love for others. We are, if you will, of the Yin and Yang of being fierce and kind. As you may know, in ancient Chinese philosophy, Yin and Yang reflect the universe and how the duality of opposing thoughts, emotions, or frequencies creates all that is to be. Yin and Yang are represented as a circle divided into two by a curving S line. One side is black and the other white. Within the black side is a small dot of white, and within the white side is a small dot of black. Although Yin and Yang are two, they are one as well. Each lives within the other. All of us are part of a forever spiral changing universe (which is represented in the Yin and Yang outer circle), and with our opposing and contrasting forces, which in essence prove to be complementary to one another and the universe, we create our world. We all must have the opposing forces of Yin (which include the feminine, intuitive, passive, night, and softness) and Yang (which include the masculine, logical, active, day, and hardness) to create balance and harmony within our world. This applies to all life, whether dragon, human, or animals (pets included)! Just think about it for a moment. Think of a day that you were experiencing great happiness. What do you think allowed you to be happy? Was it the actual events taking place? Yes, to a certain extent. Yet, somewhere in your life didn't you experience great sadness? It was your knowledge of sadness that enlightened your recognizing sense of happiness. Remember we must know dark to have light and we must know self-doubt to have self-trust. Yin and Yang rule!

Although dragons may be fierce at times (due to protecting those and that which needs to be protected) we smile with our fierceness because we trust ourselves to know that our love and kindness are being given to the universe (which is you). Although European dragons may be depicted as violent, fire-breathing, and threatening, I am of Eastern descent and was born long before humans became a part of the earth (the universe). I am ageless and forever full of strength, excellent health, wisdom, laughter, gratitude, love, kindness, compassion, and courage. I've even been told I am a very good-looking dragon! Of course, I am old and wise enough to know that beauty is in the eye of the beholder! For within me, too, you will find benevolence in all that I do and represent. Like you, I am part of the Yin and Yang club, and I have the forces of fierce determination and compassion that allow me to do my very best at all times. The same is true for all dragons. How many dragons are there in the universe? The same as how many humans there are on earth.

There is a dragon that lives within my dear Anita's heart and soul. I have helped steer her toward love, kindness, compassion, and courage. As I mentioned before Anita met me through a dream (a dimension where time and space do not exist). Unlike humans, dragons are everywhere at all times. We are pure energy. Pure empowering energy I should say! Remember quantum physics? There's a lot to it in more ways than one. Wouldn't you agree? I only wish to remind you of a few aspects of it. First, everything and everyone is created by energy. Second, energy is not subject to time and space. It is connected to all energies. It does not need to worry about the speed of light. Communication between energies is instantaneous and simultaneous no matter the distance between them. Third, energy can be in the form of frequency or matter (particles). It all depends on the observer's perception (thoughts). Fourth, an observer's thoughts and beliefs will attract like energy. The energy we emit around and through us is already connected to the universe (because we are the universe) and will draw in the same energy. Good or bad because there are no false truths in the quantum field. It is a field where infinite possibilities may be given to us by our thoughts and beliefs. This is where dragons come into play (both literally and figuratively) in your world! We are here to be set free from the dark waters and to rise up into the air (light waters) where we can be of service to you. We all need to come out.

Chapter 2

Anita Aiki Dragon

A Father's Gift

At this time, I would like to introduce you to my dear Anita. I am not really too sure where to begin with telling you about her. Let me think now. I know. I will tell you about her spirit of what makes her be. Later, we can discuss Anita's life journey. First, she is very shy. Oy vey! That'll be the day! Just a little dragon humor for you! Now, all kidding aside, even as a child, everyone knew when dear Anita was in the room. She was and is a positive mass of high spiral energy that spins to and fro smoothly and swiftly in all directions. Her energy is like that of a powerful hurricane that can cover land, air, and sea. Unlike a hurricane, though, her energy has no destructive force. Yes, her energy is very much alive and moves from one realm to another realm to another, without a moment's notice. Believe it or not her thoughts and ideas move so consistently and compassionately that she is not always aware of their speed. She is aware, though, of their momentousness. This is a quality of self-trust. Anita has never listened to the word "no." She's listened a million times over to the word "know," but never to the word "no." As a little girl, before kindergarten age, her mother made Anita mad by refusing to let her do something, and Anita did not like being told no. So Anita decided she would disappear. Her mother was a seamstress and had a Singer sewing machine that had a small brown wooden cover. Anita's mother was always using the sewing machine, so the cover remained off and to the side. Anita hid within the small cover. She has always had the ability to shape herself (whether physically or spiritually) to that which surrounds her. Her mother had no idea where she was and called the police. The police came and Anita stayed hidden. She did not come out until long after the police were gone. She came out when the no became a yes. The beginning of her perseverance.

Dear Anita's father was a very hardworking man. He worked two full-time jobs and then late at night he apprenticed to be a jeweler. What this meant to Anita, as a little girl, was that her father didn't get home until 11:00 every night. It also, at this early age, conveyed to her the importance of time. The quality of time spent together. Every night, when Anita's father got home, he would read the story of Pinocchio to her. Through her father and Pinocchio, dear Anita learned the importance of honesty and integrity. She was not going to be a jackass (like little Alexander the donkey in Pinocchio). In Pinocchio, there were many important themes. The two that had the most profound meaning to Anita were "always let your conscience be your guide" and "prove yourself brave, truthful, and unselfish, and someday you will be a real boy." Now, in Anita's case the "real boy" needs to read as the "real compassionate warrior." You will see what I mean by a real compassionate warrior later on in this book. Also, Anita learned from her father the importance of learning. Her father was always giving her little books to read. Even on yoga. Which she read! Her father, even when he read Pinocchio, would speak of and quote Confucius. Now, dear Anita was not too sure then who Confucius was, but she knew if her father liked him that she did too! Anita's father was not a wealthy man in dollars, but he was rich beyond any earthly dollars when it came to his heart and those he loved. He lavished Anita with truths, passions, imagination, unconditional love, and the quest for knowledge that would open doors to new worlds in her future. Her father's wealth found its way into dear Anita's heart before he finished the first paragraph in Pinocchio! In return, Anita gave her father the gift of devotion. Remember, Anita's father's wealth was his heart. His heart was so giving that the devotion she gave to him he blessed and returned to her in such a loving manner that it allowed dear Anita to share the same devotion in every aspect, every thought, every energy, and every life force (humans, animals, the five elements, and spiritual) that she may need for her life's journey.

Chapter 3

Little Anita

Two Immigrants and a Little Girl

Now, my friends, let me begin to tell you of my dear Anita's life's journey. Remember the song, "Do, Re, Mi" and the lyrics "Let's start at the very beginning. A very good place to start"? Anita loves the Do, Re, Mi song. So, in her honor, we will start at the very beginning. Anita's parents, Senor y la Senorita Arango, came to the United States from Cuba. Anita's father, Antonio, came first and settled in New York City. A short time later, his wife, Angelina, followed. They were so young to come to a foreign country alone and neither spoke English. Few Cubans were immigrating before Fidel Castro overturned Cuba. Anita's parents, especially her father, were very proud to be Cuban. Cubans were healthy, smart, driven, honest, principled, political, and proud people! Her parents came to the United States to find opportunities. Angelina had been a successful dressmaker and seamstress in Cuba and quickly found a job in a factory. Antonio found work in the jewelry district and apprenticed as a jewelry maker to learn the trade. They worked for two years before Anita was born. Dear Anita, Miss Ana Valentina Arango, was born in Manhattan on Valentine's Day. The day of love. And she was surrounded by the love of her parents. Anita also celebrated a second birthday each year. It would be her name day—Santa Ana. Sweetly, dear Anita did not realize that Valentine's Day was a day celebrated by all those in love. She believed, through a child's eyes, that all the celebrations, chocolates, flowers, and balloons were especially for her! That everyone was celebrating her birthday! When she became old enough to realize it was not so, it did not matter to her because she was growing up in a home that was always filled with lots of celebrations! Love, loving parents, good friends, laughter, music, and parties became a way of life for dear Anita. FYI…it warms Anita's heart when someone of old calls to wish her a happy birthday!

As a boy and young man, Anita's father was shuffled from place to place due to his mother being a concert pianist. He never had a bedroom that he could call his own much less a home. As a grown man, it was meaningful and imperative that he provide himself, his wife, and his baby daughter with a strong, stable family home. A home with a permanent address filled with life, love, humor, philosophy, education, intellectual freedom, security, understanding, and compassion. Which he provided. Dear Anita was a very lucky and blessed soul, indeed!

Anita's mother and father missed their families in Cuba and would travel back from time to time. Anita enjoyed going to Cuba. It was a place of wonderment, belonging, love, excitement, and adventure! On her first trip to Cuba, Anita met her beloved grandmother, Abuela Ana. Abuela Ana was a powerful woman surrounded by God and spirituality. Anita, as far as she can remember, always had a spiritual connection with her grandmother. Within Abuela Ana, there were special powers and a heart that overflowed with kindness and generosity. Abuela Ana loved to hold and hug Anita. And with those hugs, Abuela Ana embraced and surrounded Anita with God's light and removed adverse spirits that may try to harm her. Abuela Ana told dear Anita that she, too, had special powers and a kind and generous heart. Warmth and love were always in abundance around the two of them. Soon you will understand how a diamond shall turn into a heavenly star due to the power of such love and admiration.

Anita and her parents loved all their Cuban family and friends, and their goal was to return one day to Cuba permanently. For almost two years, Antonio and Angelina through hard work, commitment, and emotions of love and gratitude were able to live the successful American Dream of opportunity. They worked hard and were able to gain wealth in the forms of dollars (which they saved), personal belongings, and growing love for each other as a young couple, laughter, good meals, music, celebrations, and happiness. At the end of nearly two years with their trunks packed with all their belongings and saved money, the Arangos boarded the plane for what they thought would be their welcome home trip to Cuba. Upon arriving in Cuba, though, the trunks felt light. Antonio lifted them high in the air, and Angelina knew what it meant without a word having been spoken. Everything they worked so hard for had been stolen.

One thing you must realize about dear Anita's father is that he was a warrior of mind. He never allowed himself, or those he loved, to be a victim of circumstances. Yes, somebody or somebodies had stolen their worldly goods, but that was all. There was still a strong mind going on in Antonio's body. A mind that held knowledge, wisdom, compassion, love, forgiveness, today's dream for tomorrow's life, and most importantly his philosophy that "happiness is a state of mind." He, his wife, and philosophy returned once more to the United States to begin their second life of new opportunities.

Chapter 4

Dear Anita

A Young, Truthful to Self Warrior

Dear Anita, as I had mentioned before, was a little girl with lots of energy. She was full of liveliness and spirit. She was always in motion. Her mother was forever trying to keep up with her and remain focused on her given tasks at hand. After Anita's birth, her mother began to work from home. She created beautiful dresses for the ladies of the neighborhood and dear Anita. Fortunately, for both Anita and her mother, dear Anita had a little friend named Selena. They were both about the same age. Selena was a little girl who Anita's mother found all alone on the street one day. You see, Selena's mother had to work and had no place to leave her except on the street to play. In the afternoon, after work, Selena's mother would return and they would go back home. Anita's mother met with Selena's mother and it was decided that Selena would remain with Anita during the day. The two girls had great fun playing! They would laugh and sing songs and make up games to play. What was very interesting was Selena was Chinese and knew no Spanish or English. Anita only knew Spanish. Yet, they communicated and had fun. The two little girls through their innocence and imagination effortlessly and spontaneously created a world of their own language and happiness. A world filled, too, with laughter, laughter, and more laughter.

Unbeknownst to Anita, at this time, this, through Selena, was her first introduction to me, Aiki Dragon. It began with the laughter. Remember, we dragons love laughter. How about a little laughter now? Do you know why dragons often sleep during the day? So they can keep an eye on the knights! Drum roll, please! And dragons love music too. Anita and Selena's songs were beautiful music to my ears! Sweet, energetic voices sending out love to the universe!

Around this time, my dear Anita decided she wanted to experience flying with her tricycle! It was a very pretty tricycle. It was all red and shiny. And like Anita, it was ready to go for an adventure. So, Anita, being a respectful little girl to her mother, informed her that she was going outside to fly. Anita's mother was busy making a dress and not totally listening and replied, "Okay, go have fun." Dear Anita, being told to have fun, set out to do just that. She and her tricycle went out on the landing of the second-story apartment building and prepared for her flight into the sky. Anita sat down squarely on the seat, started pedaling as fast as she could, and the fire-red tricycle took flight to the heavens. At first, anyway. Fortunately, dear Anita, in her child's wisdom, had the foresight to "blast off" from above the staircase that leads to the first floor, which helped, in a way, to break her fall. Or maybe I should say, helped to break her crown. Anita and her tricycle began to spiral and tumble down to the ground. Going down, Anita hit her head hard and split open her forehead at the third eye level. Actually, it opened her third eye! Now, during this time, Anita's mother heard the sound of the tricycle's engines, if you will, and she did some taking off herself, running out the front door to Anita. Her mother placed salt directly to Anita's head wound (this was a form of healing that she had learned from Abuela Ana). Anita, with her high energy, and tricycle were off to other adventures almost immediately! Unbeknownst to Anita, this was her second introduction to me. She desired to fly like a dragon out into the world. Who do you think put that idea into her head? Me! The human may have gotten slightly hurt, but it allowed the spirituality of the third eye to open. Of course, my dear Anita has self-trust and the courage of a dragon, which allowed her to have the momentary awareness of a dragon's flight.

Sometimes, dear Anita's adventures were not always of the high-flying magnitude. There was a time when her mother was in the bathroom crying. Anita did not know why her mother was crying, but she could feel her pain and sorrow. Later, she found out that her mother had lost a baby at birth. Time has revealed that the baby may have been born alive and sold illegally by hospital staff. Anita also was aware of the times that her mother was alone in their home frightened, lonely, and full of sorrow. Anita's mother would tell her stories of having been followed by men. Again, dear Anita could feel her pain. It was at this time that Anita's compassion became wide awake and she vowed to protect her mother and family. Within a year or so Anita would take on more family responsibilities, due to her father working so many hours and her mother not speaking English. One of the first family duties she performed was calling the plumber. The plumber hung up thinking she was playing. She called back and using a deeper, prominent voice made it clear she was not playing. Dear Anita practiced using this voice over and over, with herself, so that moving forward others knew instantly that she meant business. Dear Anita took her job as the young head of the house seriously. She was a young warrior of truth and compassion. A samurai who was learning the importance of being of service.

The young warrior, dear Anita, was called upon once more when she experienced her first true sense of personal sorrow while in Cuba.

This sorrow was not one like the type she had experienced through her mother's sorrows. No, this was her sorrow and her little heart was huge with grief. Cuba's government was now under the leadership of Fidel Castro. The country's attitude toward the United States had quickly changed and not in a positive manner. The government supporters' shouts and cries were "Yankees, Go Home." Those from America were no longer being welcomed in Cuba. Anita was aware this would be her last visit to Cuba for many years. She had to say goodbye to all she knew there. She had to say goodbye to a lifestyle that was filled with love, happiness, endless adventures, and Abuela Ana. A little girl's heart was breaking into a million pieces. Yet, within each of those million pieces of broken heart was a million pieces of Abuela Ana's love. Love that would bring the heart back as one with a trillion little hearts of love within it. In the face of despair or fear, a compassionate warrior must have courage. On the flight back to the United States, Anita, with sorrow in her heart, wondered about her world. There was so much of her life still in Cuba, and now with the United States coming closer and closer again to her, she was lost as to where she belonged. With Abuela Ana's love in her heart, dear Anita would discover that she had the courage to start a brand-new life in the United States (which would reach up high into the universe).

Now, warriors, like dragons, can also be fierce when needed. And there was such a time in dear Anita's young life that she needed to be strong and protect her integrity. Anita had just returned for the last time from visiting her beloved Abuela Ana in Cuba, and while there she spent many days outdoors running and playing with other kids and swimming in the ocean, which caused her skin to darken. Upon returning to New York, she went, for the first time by herself, to the neighboring park. She felt so grown-up to be able to go alone and excited to play with other kids (like she had done in Cuba). Once she got to the park, there was a boy, named Larry, around Anita's age who told her she could not play with him and the other kids because she was a "spic." Although Anita did not know what a spic was, she knew by his harsh tone that it was not a good thing. It hurt her that someone could be so unkind and mean. Due to Larry's comment, none of the other kids wanted anything to do with her, either. Confused and hurt Anita ran home crying to her mother. When Anita got home and explained what had happened, her mother responded, in Spanish, "Larry is no better or worse than you, and you must learn to defend yourself." After this, she closed the front door, leaving Anita outside by herself.

Dear Anita felt so alone and isolated. The neighborhood kids didn't want to play with her because she was Cuban (or a *spic* as Larry put it) and her mother had closed her out of the house where she had always been surrounded by love. Plus, her loving Abuela Ana was nowhere near to give her guidance. Anita sat and pondered all the emotions that were swelling in her. She became centered in all that was around her. Suddenly, she knew what needed to be done! She got up and ran back to the park. She confronted Larry, in front of the other kids, and punched him in the face. She had caught Larry by surprise and he fell to the ground crying. Then she ran back home and continued to ponder the day's events. At that young age, Anita realized that she was not liked because she was Cuban and not Jewish like most of the other kids. Thinking to herself, she questioned, how could they not like her? They don't even know who she is! Being a young warrior of compassion, she did not hold their discrimination toward her against them. Instead, she realized that she must educate them about Cubans. She must introduce them to the wonderful world of being Cuban. Dear Anita discovered a new friend that day. The friend's name was "Action." Action had taught her to not judge or complain about a situation, but to move forward toward a win-win solution. Action allowed success to be on her side.

Anita went on to make friends with the kids from the park. She formed a group with them and called it "The Arango Routes." She opened her Cuban world of pride, honesty, music, laughter, Cuban foods, and parties. She taught them how to play games like Boys Capture Girls. This game has significance because although it is a child's game, it mimics a battlefield setting. You have two opposing sides that aim to capture (not to hurt or harm) the other side and place them in jail. The side that captures all of the other sides is the winner. Another battlefield-like game Anita taught them was Ring-A-Levio. This one was more of a strategic game on how to break the weakest link. Two sides of about eight individuals each would interlink their arms tightly around each other, with the stronger players in the middle, and face the opposite side (which was about thirty yards away). Each team would take turns in calling out who they wanted from the other team. The named player had to come charging toward them and attempt to break the tight hold. If they did not break it, they would become a player on their team. Keep in mind all this was played on top of concrete. It was not unusual for people to get hurt and even be sent to the hospital. Due to Anita evolving more and more into a compassionate warrior, this game was not played for long. In fact, soon after Anita stopped suggesting they play Ring-A-Levio, it became outlawed! Boys Capture Girls was most popular because it allowed dear Anita to use her compassionate warrior skills to not harm but to disarm her opponent through love and kindness. And in case you may be wondering, dear Anita was never captured. She had too much movement of spirit!

Remember Anita's mother had closed the door and left her outside? Although Anita was feeling temporarily unloved, at that moment, her mother was surrounding her with love from a distance. Her mother by shutting a physical door allowed Anita to open her inner door of how to be true to her own self and actions. Love has always been around Anita. Always. And in case you are wondering about Larry, his mother came shortly after the punch in the face incident to talk with Anita's mother. Larry's mother wanted to know what kind of girl her mother was raising. I would say that Anita's mother and father were raising a well-centered girl who had the fierceness of a dragon and the heart of a warrior.

Like all little girls, Anita had to go to school. She attended kindergarten and first grade in public school. Anita would cry when having to go to school. She didn't know English and the teachers didn't know Spanish. The teachers were indifferent to her. There were no special non-English programs for her to become enrolled in so she could learn at a more appropriate level. With the language barrier, she was unable to learn what was being taught. The teachers would call her mother and tell her that Anita needed to dress more like a student. The teachers criticized that her dresses were too pretty and were more for parties than school. Now keep in mind, Anita's mother was a successful dressmaker and she made all Anita's clothes herself, stitch by stitch. They were beautiful clothes and originals! In second grade, Anita began Catholic school. Poor little thing, she still did not know English, at this time, and the nuns, like the public school teachers, did not know Spanish. Nor, unfortunately, did they care to learn Spanish. Anita would continue to cry when having to go to school and she would lay her head on her desk in despair. Anita had the passion to learn, but the nuns were not willing to teach her. Instead of seeing a willing and ready to learn child, they chose to see a non-English-speaking problem child. They did not care to understand that everyone, no matter what age or language they speak, is their own soul with their own thoughts, enthusiasm, and self-worth. Anita had been taught well by her father to be confident, honest, and have integrity. Thus this is how she behaved with the nuns. Alas, though, they perceived her as being ornery and rebellious. The nuns would have their rulers and ask Anita to hold out her hands so they could be swatted. The first time she held out her hands, she did not know what was going to happen. Once she learned, she refused to do it again and her attitude was *catch me if you can*. I ask you, is that being ornery and rebellious or is that having self-respect and integrity?

Through her driving force of perseverance, Anita did learn English and this helped in her schooling. It did not change the nuns' attitude, but it changed Anita in the respect that with English the door had been opened so she could learn. Even at this early age studying was important to Anita. At home, she would study, study, study. She could hear the other kids playing and laughing, but she would stay with her books and learn. The decision to study so intensely and steadfastly was hers and hers alone. And she had the loving support of her family with her studying. Her mother always emphasized that she could do it. That she could do anything. Her father was a scholar of his own right. He was an avid reader who was very philosophical and political. He had an eternal passion for knowledge and intellectual growth. It gave him joy to see his daughter's commitment to her studying and aspiration to be the best she could be.

During Catholic school, her sense of humor began to come through. Humor was a great way to cancel out or defuse any negative situation that may be going on around her. One of her favorite phrases to use, which was told to her by her father, was "I see, said the blind man!" Of course, there were times of humor with Anita's behavior in Catholic school. Like the time when she chased a boy! It was the Christmas play and little Gary was supposed to kiss Anita in the play. Being a little boy, he was shy of girls, and Anita, being Anita, was shy of no one, and when he refused to kiss her, she became determined to get that kiss. She chased him around and around the auditorium. He was screaming no and she was screaming yes! You see, the kiss was in the script; therefore, in following the rules, the kiss must happen. Needless to say, Anita and the boy kissed! Although humorous, this is another instance where Anita's perseverance paid off!

As a growing young girl, Anita had the desire to become a missionary. She wanted to go to a faraway continent like Asia or Africa so she could help and be of service to others. The warrior in her was becoming stronger. Remember, Abuela Ana's love lived in Anita's heart and through this love she had courage. Anita had no fear to leave home and travel to another continent. From her days in Cuba, Anita had observed that her Abuela Ana was a healer and helped those in need. Inherently, from her Abuela Ana, Anita had the same attributes and she wanted to reach out to help those who may be impoverished, sickly, or in need of learning. She wanted them to live in a healthier and better-educated world. Dear Anita envisioned herself as a little girl of God dressed in white. A white illuminated by love's pure light. She reached out to many different organizations and requested information be sent to her. Brochures and pamphlets were sent to Anita, but her mother was fearful that harm may come to her; therefore, she hid all the correspondence. Unfortunately, Anita did not become the missionary that she had envisioned, but she never lost sight of helping others. Abuela Ana's healing heart and hands would only be a thought away when the time came for Anita to be at one with those in need.

Anita became of junior high school age, and through the advice of a family friend, Anita switched back to the New York public school system. Public school gave Anita wonderful freedom from the strict policy and procedures of Catholic school, but it was a wild and dangerous school environment. It was so dangerous that grade levels stayed with grade levels. Anita was in the seventh grade and the seventh graders were confined to their side of the school. For safety sake, they did not mix with the other grade levels. The school was built of brick and cement and surrounded with a tall chain-link fence which both kept people in and out. Anita began to see a treacherous world where danger lurked around every corner. Fights would ensue on the school grounds and in the restrooms. Fights that would include fists and knives. Dear Anita did some fast growing up during these times. She learned to carry a switchblade. A little startling to hear, isn't it? Keep in mind, though, she is a compassionate warrior. Her main goal is to protect herself and those who may be harming her from harm. She protects all with love, kindness, and a great sense of humor. Although, during this time, Abuela Ana was in Cuba, she continued to live in Anita's heart and give Anita courage and protection. Anita had no fear. In the background of her mind, she could hear her mother's words "you are no better or less than anyone" and "you must defend yourself." She knew, too, from Larry and her friend "Action" that she must take charge and do whatever is necessary, in a positive and loving manner, to keep her safety and integrity. She also had the Old World knowledge of her father and carried his core beliefs regarding the importance of education (of self and others) and self-trust.

Amidst the fighting and switchblades, Anita remained an avid student. Her names Ana and Arango began with A's and that is what she got in her classes. She would accept nothing less than an A. She also loved the number nine; therefore, only grades in the nineties and higher were permissible to her. She worked hard and put in the time and was rewarded with straight A's for all of her courses. The same was not true, though, when it came to conduct. Anita had all her high energy and sense of integrity, which would spin like a wild wind throughout the land of school. It was important to Anita that she have a voice even if it meant not getting A's in conduct. Needless to say, she did not receive A's in conduct. She received D's and F's. Anita was a smart young girl and she decided to develop her own philosophy regarding D's and F's. As she would tell her parents, D's stood for delightful and F's for fantastic. The only thing was the school's philosophy and Anita's philosophy regarding conduct grades were not the same. The dean of the school called her parents and informed them that D's and F's were not, by their standards, what Anita claimed them to be. Unsurprisingly, her parents were not amused and the school's philosophy overruled Anita's. But never fear, Anita kept her high energy and voice, and conduct grades would be what they would be.

As you know warriors must keep their bodies well-tuned. As a little girl, Anita used to run and play in the park with her friends, and this made her strong. Now that she was in junior high school she did her physical education activities in the school gym. Part of her exercise routine was known as the "jailhouse workout." This type of workout includes push-ups, pull-ups, squats, and lunges. Just like studying her books, Anita was faithful to her exercising. At the end of the school year, she won the John F. Kennedy Youth Physical Fitness Program certificate for the best physically fit student. Anita's mind and body were working as one as she ran swiftly up the warrior's road of empowerment.

Chapter 5

Young Anita

A Mindful Warrior

The warrior's road was clearing itself for dear Anita to spread her wings in the workforce. She was born in the Chinese year of the Dragon and the hour of the Tiger. Dragons are pure energy, independent and strong and always confident and enthusiastic in their thoughts and actions. Tigers are active and courageous and always enjoy challenges and excitement. Tigers also are guardians of children. Around the time of junior high school, on the weekends, after her studying was done, Anita began to babysit a young couple's two adopted children. She took great pride in seeing that they were well taken care of under her watch. The watchful eye of a tiger. So much laughter and childhood games overflowed in her rapport with the young ones. The humor and playfulness of a dragon. Oh, my dear, dear Anita, how I love you and your kindness to others. A dragon has her wings!

Then came the mighty fine time of working at the five-and-dime! You didn't know dragons could make rhymes too, did you? Well, we can! We love music, and music is words set in rhymes and rhythms.

Dear Anita's first outside job was at Woolworth's, where she was a stock person. She placed newly received items on the store shelves for customers to look over and buy. It was through a friend of her mother's that she was able to get this job at such a tender young age. School still came first, though. Once work was done she was back home doing her studies. Anita enjoyed being in the workforce, being around people, and earning money. The money she earned was hers to spend as she liked. For this she was very grateful. What dear Anita did not like was her actual job of being a stocker. It was a dirty job in the sense that boxes that the items came in, as well as the items and shelves, were covered in dust and dirt. She asked for a different position and was given the job of a cashier, which proved to be another dirty job due to the grit and grime on the coins and dollar bills. Anita continued to work, though, because the job gave her the qualities of independence and freedom. Remember, dragons love their freedom! It also allowed Anita to grasp the concept of being accurate and accountable for money. If her cash drawer was short, she had to pay the difference out of her hard-earned money. She learned the principles of math very quickly and saw to it all monies coming in and out of her cash drawer were to the penny. Also, dear Anita learned how important an education was to one's future. Without an education, she may be cashiering for a long time. Studying remained her top priority.

During junior high, Anita made time for lots of friends and Donny (a boyfriend or as she puts it a kissing buddy). Unlike Gary from the school Christmas play, she didn't have to chase Donny! Donny was the singer in a band. A funny story is that Donny needed a place to practice with his group, so Anita told him to come over to her home. He, the group members, and loudspeakers came over. The guys were hoisting the huge and heavy speakers up to the second floor just as Anita's father was coming home after a long day of work. Mr. Arango took a look at the speakers, the guys, and then Anita. He gave Anita an all-knowing Confucius kind of smile, said nothing, and went inside. He knew this would bring Anita happiness and he trusted her judgment. Let the music begin!

Soon Anita began high school. Her high school years were similar to junior high in regard to the knives and fights. No fears though had Anita, for she had an "open mind" attitude that allowed her to develop further her sense of awareness regarding her surroundings and the people within it. Her reaction skills to another's thoughts and movements were being sharpened and on target. This was wonderful and natural training for a compassionate warrior. Music continued to revolve in Anita's sphere. She loved the sounds of the Beach Boys, Pink Floyd, The Doors, and The Beatles. Music can tell one so much of another's personality and life force. Think about it. Songs like Pink Floyd's "Astronomy Domine," "Set the Controls for the Heart of the Sun," and "Interstellar Overdrive" all have a futuristic tone of reaching out to the universe and the remembering of a lesson learned. The Beach Boys with "Good Vibrations," "God Only Knows," and "Fun, Fun, Fun" are songs about making connections with others and how they make us feel happiness and delight. Of course, "Fun, Fun, Fun" sings of a young lady with a fast car and blaring music. Anita loves a fast car that plays loud music! Believe it or not, Anita's first car was a white Trans Am with T-tops (which she removed whether it was hot or cold outside…thank goodness for a car's heater!). She had fun, fun, fun with that speed demon! Or maybe I should call it that speed dragon, because it soared with the swiftness and grace of a dragon in flight to new adventures and had wisdom for moments of deep thoughts! Of all the songs she listened to, her favorite was "I Want to Hold Your Hand" by The Beatles. For her, this was a song of pure love, joy, and romance. Music has always made Anita smile with love and happiness and excitement. All of which multiplies her energy by a hundredfold. If you add dancing, you will create a whirlwind of energy and joy that will spin forever and a day!

Also, around this time, dear Anita's attention was turning to include boyfriends and fashion. She was a teenage girl and had teenage girl interests! Anita left Woolworth's and took a job at a boutique. She was given a school hardship program, which allowed her to have all her classes in the morning and work in the afternoon. By noon, she was running to the boutique to work a full-time afternoon shift. She did not get off work until 9 p.m. The boutique was run by two brothers. Two very loud, argumentative, and high-tempered brothers! They were always screaming at their employees, threatening to or actually firing them. Due to Anita's high energy and sense of humor, she was not disturbed by their attitudes. The brothers' dispositions only made her laugh and work harder to sell more clothes. Nobody was going to fire her! She loved this job and all the beautiful clothes that surrounded her. She didn't get paid lots of money, but she got fantastic discounts on the clothes. On Friday's when she got paid, she would spend her paycheck on clothes. She loved clothes! Of course she did. That's the dragon in her. We love to be flamboyant, at times, and we love to be stylish at all times! Anita was a natural beauty. With her style and clothes she was (and still is) breathtaking. And the guys noticed! Anita turned the heads of the young men as she walked by them. Now, keep in mind, Anita did not just attract the guys because of her looks. No, she attracted them, as well, because of her skills of an athlete, mind of a philosopher, words of truth, and heart of kindness. FYI, Anita had more friends who were boys than girls. The girls saw her as competition, even though Anita did not view herself to be as such. Soon dating for Anita was in motion. School and work still came first, mind you. Anita's time to relax and have fun was on Saturday nights after work. A nice night out to her was usually a long, relaxing dinner with lots of conversation. Anita's mind even when relaxing was always inquisitive and wanting to learn and share knowledge. And Anita, as you know, loved music and dancing too! One of her favorite dances was (and still is) the Cha-cha-cha!

When it came to dating, dear Anita's father, in a loving and protective manner, was very strict with her. Mr. Arango had a strong ethnic, macho, Cuban streak. He had to meet, scrutinize, and approve of the young man before Anita could go out with him. Mr. Arango never encouraged her to date Latin guys because they only had one thing on their mind. He told her to "never do anything that would cause me to have to kill one of them" or "cause me to go to jail." If Mr. Arango felt a young man was being disrespectful to his daughter, he would chase him down the street and the guy would never return to their home. Anita also had a curfew, which she wisely kept. Her father with his all-knowing sense of "what boys want" would stay awake until Anita returned home from her date, on time, safe and sound.

One of the guys Anita dated was a photographer named Jeff. He took photos of the various professional groups that were playing in the city. With his concert backstage passes, he and Anita would get to see all that took place behind the scenes and meet with the singers and band members. These were exciting times for Anita. Again, music filled her world and heart. For now, this is where I need to pause the story of Jeff and Anita. We will pick up where we left off, a little later.

Anita, also during this time, began to have an interest in cars. At this young age, cars represented transportation, friends, and fun. One Saturday night, a friend of hers was staying over and they were invited to a party in Brooklyn (Anita lived in Queens). Anita wanted to go to the party; therefore, they were going! Her parents had a gold with a black hard top Buick. This was her means of transportation to the party. Never mind that she didn't have a driver's license, know how to drive, or have her parents' permission to take the car. Anita had a plan. First, she and her friend made the bed so it looked as though they were sleeping. Then they tied bedsheets together to make a rope and left out the second-story bedroom window. They got to the car, got in, and drove off. Part of dear Anita's plan was to teach herself how to drive as she was driving. While driving the car she remained focused and proceeded down the street to pick up additional friends. Things were going well until they got to the Brooklyn Bridge and then the car started shaking and rattling. It wasn't the car, though. It was the construction of the road on the Brooklyn Bridge that caused the car to behave as it did. This was somewhat unsettling, but Anita remained focused and calm. Once off the bridge all was fine. Anita and her friends made it to the party and had fun. They came back across the Brooklyn Bridge and the car started shaking and rattling again. All was fine, though. Anita dropped off the group of friends and she and her friend went back home after having parked the car. They climbed the bedsheets and fell asleep for a few minutes. Suddenly, there was a lot of commotion going on down the hall. Anita got up and went to investigate. It appears that the neighborhood busybody had called the police to report the car stolen. Everybody went to the car to meet with the police. The neighbor was telling the police how she saw two men get into the car and drive off with it. To themselves, the police and Anita's parents were thinking how odd that the car had been stolen and returned all in the same night, albeit in a different parking spot. Plus, there had been no forced entry into the car. Anita didn't say a word (for once)! I would say, though, that she has the mischief and tenacity of a dragon!

Now, just so you know, Anita did finally get her driver's license and moving forward did get her parents' permission to drive the family car. It was a hardship, though, because everyone needed the car. Anita asked her parents to help her buy a car, but they simply did not have the funds. Anita's father recommended that she ask her godfather, who was of great means, for a loan. Anita called her godfather and explained why she needed a car and asked him for a $5,000 loan. He told her no. Anita continued to drive the family car. Many, many years later,

Anita's godfather called her and explained that he was deaf and had lost not only his hearing, but his wealth as well. He asked if he could have $5,000 to which she replied yes. A warrior's unconditional love and compassion has no boundaries, hesitancies, or memories of the past when it comes to helping others in need. A million blessings to dear Anita!

Now, cars have always been very important and spiritual to Anita. As I mentioned previously, cars represented transportation, fun, and friends to Anita (and still do), but as high school continued on she began to have a new sensation for cars. A car was beginning to represent a form of departure for her. Not the usual way of departure in the sense of getting away from, but more in the sense of taking away with. Let me take a few moments and explain what I mean. Dear Anita had a beautiful home life that overflowed with love, support, celebrations, and philosophical words of wisdom. Yet, in all that abundancy she did not have a room that she could call her own. Once in the car, alone, she was able to have her own room, which allowed her to take away with her her world of love. Driving, unbeknownst to her at the time, was an act of meditation where she would relax her mind and become centered and at one with herself. She had the private time and space to contemplate her thoughts, words, dreams, and personal visions. It was a form of relaxation and recreation as well. A car gave Anita swiftness and speed, thus allowing her to extend her high energy with just the lightest touch to the gas pedal. The turning of the steering wheel allowed Anita to solidly spin the car around from one direction to another, as needed. Can you see the correlation of the driving of the car and a warrior's skills? A car also gave dear Anita a new sense of future direction. The car eventually led her to many trips to the airport, where she would park the car, for hours, and watch the planes take off and land. She could become one with the planes and feel the sensations of taking off into the sky and heading to new destinations. Likewise, she could become one with the landing planes and feel the earth under her feet and the serenity of being of the land. Driving home, Anita would begin to feel the warmth of her parents' generosity and love flow into her heart with smiles and the knowledge that family and home are with you always. What a beautiful forever world!

Anita was now graduating high school, a semester early, due to the school's hardship program and her commitment to studying. Proudly she graduated with honors. Anita knew it was time for a new chapter in her life and she decided that it should begin at the Pan Am building. The many trips she took to the airport watching the planes take off and land made her realize that she wanted to be part of the traveling world. Don't forget, she had at one time wanted to be a missionary and travel to Asia or Africa. Anita applied to be a flight attendant. For Anita, this would be a wise and safe, adventurous way to travel to other places. Also, the business mind of Anita knew that being a flight attendant would allow her to be paid for her travels and adventures. Plus, she could be of service to people while in the air. Unfortunately, the airlines did not have the same thoughts as Anita and they did not choose to bring her on board. Anita continued to take her drives to the airport, watch the planes take off and land, and contemplate what may lie ahead for her. Like a dragon she never gets discouraged. She may reside in her ocean of thoughts for a while, but those thoughts have power and she'll be in the sky taking flight soon. Both figuratively and literally!

Meanwhile, Anita decided to enroll in St. John's University. At this stage of her life, she really wasn't in the know regarding colleges, but in high school she had seen other students with university and college brochures, so she knew, at least for now, this was the route she should take. St. John's University was in Queens, near where she lived, and this allowed her the flexibility to continue dating Jeff. She went one semester and then she, Jeff, and a group of friends decided to travel Europe. She paid for her plane ticket and then told her parents she was going. Needless to say, they were surprised, but it was not in their nature to hold their daughter back from a life's adventure. With their blessings and her own money Anita left with Jeff and their friends to travel Europe.

Europe was proving to be a wonderful experience for dear Anita. She had excitement and wonderment in exploring a new world. The days were spent hiking the Northern Downs of England and the nights reading the *Hobbit* trilogy by campfire. From her father's Chinese philosophy, she knew that life could be uncertain and that life could be full of surprises. So far, this new life and world had given Anita a new sense of freedom. For the first time in Anita's life, time was not dictated in hours, minutes, and seconds. Time, like her, was high energy. It encompassed every aspect of her life, but there was no restriction to it. Time flowed smoothly like the stream in a creek rolling over pebbles in unison with the wind blowing through the trees. Time moved gracefully and at its own speed. It had no beginning and no end. And this is how Anita felt. She was at one with time, nature, life, and herself. She traveled with the harmony of time's civility through England and Germany. One evening, while dancing in Germany, she met a man who was of a Venezuelan and German descent and a few years older than Anita. There was an instant bond of friendship between the two of them. That same evening, Geraldo asked Anita if she would like to travel and explore the countryside and new places with him. The adventurer in Anita made the varoom sound of a racing motorcycle and yelled out like an announcer at a car race an emphatic and solid yes!

Chapter 6

Learning Anita

Life has uncertainties. Life has surprises.

Adventure in motion! That's how life was now going for Anita. Traveling and exploring with Geraldo was sporty and on the go. Dear Anita held Geraldo as one of her dearest friends. He had so many interests to which Anita could relate. He was a man who loved fast cars and motorcycles. So did Anita! He was a person of politics. So was Anita! He was a man who loved to travel. So was Anita! During their time of friendship, Anita and he did a trip to Costa del Sol in Spain. She had longed to go there (her father had often stated they were from there!). What an exciting and venturesome three weeks they had in Costa del Sol. The hiking of the land. The exploration of small fishing towns. The driving of the roads on an Italian-made Moto Guzzi motorcycle (known for its racing success). This is when dear Anita began to drive motorcycles. Not only was Geraldo a great friend, but he had turned into her driving instructor. He taught her single-handedly how to speed the roads with precision and care. Anita loved the wind in her face. They would race their motorcycles down the countryside. The motorcycles would take them to beautiful beaches of sand, waters, and sun. Lots of sun! Anita tanned very darkly during those three weeks. So dark that when she left Spain to return to Germany, the officials did not believe that the picture on her passport and she were the same person. After much continuous and convincing talk, Anita was able to make it back to Germany.

In returning to Germany, Geraldo went back to work at BMW. He was a professional car racer and test-drove BMWs. If you will pardon the pun, cars and Geraldo made a strong impact on each other. Cars for Geraldo were life! Geraldo for cars was the one who gave them life. His dexterity in handling the wheel and road allowed them to soar at speeds that the average person or automobile would never know. It made for him to be one of the top test drivers for BMW! Geraldo was the friend who taught Anita how to drive professional sports cars. Around and around the speedway laps they would go with the speed of a dragon's wings in flight and Confucius's wisdom to keep them safe!

Geraldo was also a political activist who shot documentaries regarding the demoralization of Communism. Anita could relate to the downheartedness of Communism. For it was Communism that had been keeping her beloved Abuela Ana and her separated for many years. Communism prevented Anita and her family from corresponding with her grandmother due to the government's practice of intercepting and reading mail, bugging telephone calls, and bribing people to relinquish private information of others. There was no truthful or safe way to communicate with those in Cuba. Silently, succinctly, and with the connection to the ground, Anita and Geraldo glided, without sound, on the soil of the forbidden Communist land called East Berlin, so he could film another documentary. Anita could feel Geraldo's passion in his documentaries. These documentaries were to open the eyes of those who could not or would not choose to see the dispiriting ways of Communism. It was an expression of liberation for those who were being exploited in a dehumanizing manner. Their true inner and outer voices of who they were meant to be were being silenced and replaced with selfish and mindless words of hypocrisy. The words of Geraldo's documentaries gave the East Berlin citizens praiseworthy notoriety and voice for the world to hear! Words are always heard, even though they may not be immediately listened to due to fear, oppression, prejudices, or by not taking the time to learn another's plight! Documentaries such as Geraldo's were trailblazers in the gift of opening East Berlin and its people to a once-again thriving land where a person's life and voice may be encircled joyously by self-trust, the trust of others, and freedom to be who they chose to be! Similarly, the same freedom was given to the proud citizens of dear Anita's much-loved Cuba! Aleluya, Cuba, y su hermosa gente!

Anita planned to remain in Germany. She had enrolled in school and she was a translator in English. Word came, though, that her father was ill and that a passage had been provided so she may return home at once. Anita let her friend Geraldo know that she was leaving and would be returning after visiting with her father. Alas, it would prove that Anita would not be returning. Anita and Geraldo corresponded by mail for a while. He wrote her words of esteem and well wishes on his blue stationery. Over time his letters would stop coming and those that Anita had received unexpectedly disappeared, but their bond of friendship would always remain present.

Anita had been given airline tickets to New York with a stop in Paris. When the plane landed in Paris, it was Anita's wish to momentarily get off the plane so she could see Paris (even if it was just through the airport's windows). Dragons love to fly to places and explore! In her attempt to disembark the plane, she was told that she would have to remain in her seat due to Marshall Orders. The person who had purchased her airline tickets made it a requirement that she remain on board to prevent the possibility of her staying in Paris longer than she should. Dragons do not like being told no and confined to a small space, but dear Anita knew her father was ill and took this as a sign that she must hurry home. Unknown to Anita, her parents had reached out to the husband of the young couple whose children she would babysit. He had become a family friend and successful doctor. He was the one who arranged the passage for Anita to return to New York. As you will soon learn, he did not help Anita in a truthful manner as he should have. Dear Anita so young had no understanding as to how dishonesty of the mind may make lies look like truths. Sometimes the word *young* is another word for innocence. My wings were gently wrapped around Anita and no harm was to come to her. A few life lessons, yes, but no harm. I have ancient wisdom in my body and I can feel deceit long before it attempts to place harm into motion.

Once in New York, Anita returned to her father and mother. Anita's father was ill for he had missed his sweet daughter, and life without her was just too sad. Although his Confucius thinking brain told him that Anita was doing well and she was safe in Europe, his heart was crying in loneliness for her presence and of the bond of love they shared as father and daughter. Even though dear Anita was a young woman, now, in his love for her she would always remain his little girl. He, too, remembered those wonderful late nights of Pinocchio!

The doctor's name was Ronnie and he had brought Anita home to her family and most importantly to her ailing father. This was true. The love that dear Anita and her father shared only continued to grow and made her father well again. This is true. Ronnie believed that Anita had the qualities needed to become a doctor like him. The fact that Anita had the qualities needed was true. That she should be a doctor like him was not true. Ronnie convinced Anita and her family that she should become a doctor. He graciously (in appearance) set her up in her own apartment (near school and about an hour away from her parents) and enrolled her in Dowling College, which was an exclusive private college for only the wealthy few. To give you an example of the wealth, the college was held in William K. Vanderbilt's Idle Hour mansion and Anita's science classes were held on a yacht. An interesting bit of information is that their motto was Learning, Wisdom, and Compassion. Sounds like the school of a warrior, doesn't it? Studying whether on land or water was of the utmost importance to her. Although she no longer made D's (delightful) and F's (fantastic) in conduct, she continued to make A's in academics. Her mindset was still "study, study, study, and study some more." Anita looked forward to going to her classes and got along with everyone until the day of Catch the Flag.

Catch the Flag was a game Anita and the students played one afternoon. It is a game of mental strategy and physical exercise. The object of the game is to capture the flag and take it back to your territory. For this, you need a large area, which Dowling supplied, with its massive estate grounds, rolling hills, and trees. Two teams were formed (yellow and green) and each had fifteen players. Anita was on the yellow team and formulated a strategic plan of her own. She would infiltrate the green team, in plain sight, as a spy, and run with them to locate the flag. She let her other yellow team members look for the flag on their own. She was determined that her team was going to win. Sure enough, Anita was the first to spot the flag! With lightning speed, she was able to catch the flag and complete the full obstacle course of running, jumping, and climbing up the hills, with the utmost swiftness and agility. She proudly placed the flag in her team's territory and pronounced them the winners! Her team was amazed and cheering great sounds of victory. The green team and professor were not feeling the same jubilation. They were down and outright mad at Anita for having won unfairly, as they saw it, by not following the rules. Anita quite sincerely stated she had won fairly and had violated no rules. The rules and regulations were reviewed and dear Anita had spoken the truth. Nowhere in the rules does it state that a member of one team may not run with the opposite team. Anita's Catch the Flag victory was a true victory!

Ronnie let Anita be a full-time student during her first semester at Dowling. At the beginning of the second semester, he came calling for her. Through his verbal and physical innuendos, he was making it very obvious that his intentions for her were to be more than sending her to school to be a doctor. Anita was stunned. Ronnie was a dear family friend who was known as Ronnie the Doctor. He was held with high esteem and reverence by her parents. She had babysat his children and watched them grow. She was fond of and close to his wife. Anita desired no part of Ronnie's deceitful and unfaithful world. She told no one of Ronnie's deceiving ways. She was fearful that this may hurt too many people (especially her parents). Anita simply left Dowling College, the apartment, and the pursuit of being a doctor. She went into the heart of New York City and remained for approximately five years while my wings continued to embrace her in love and safety.

During these five years, dear Anita did a variety of jobs to include receptionist. Being a receptionist was not what it was supposed to be. At two of the companies (a men's hair replacement center and furniture store) where she manned the phones, the male owners wanted to manhandle her in a hustling manner. One of the owners asked her to remove her blouse if she wanted to move forward and another told her she could earn extra money as a VIP of the company. Please note that VIP did not stand for a very important person. Anita straightforwardly with humor told him and his VIP clients that if she wanted to be a prostitute, she would make a lot more money than what they were offering! Both these guys were too much like Ronnie in their requests.

Anita never forgot her father's warning about men only wanting one thing from a pretty girl. She had one word for those two guys—goodbye!

Now, don't be feeling sorry for dear Anita. She is a true warrior, and a warrior does not dwell on other people's unkind motives, become a victim, or feel sorry for themselves. A warrior learns from such obstacles and moves forward with a plan of action, which includes gathering additional strength and knowledge. The dragon in her was fierce with honor and perseverance. Anita learned the lesson that integrity was much more important than money. This valuable lesson led her to re-open a door from her past.

While working at the boutique in high school, Anita had taken on a second part-time job at a woman's health club. It was run by a woman named Lucille and she opened the first health club exclusively to women at Herald Square in New York (near Macy's flagship store). This health club offered all the amenities of a regular health club to include weights, saunas, exercise classes, and swimming with the exception of men. Women had their own place to exercise without the worry of men disrupting their workout. Exercise and money originally led Anita to work at the women's fitness club. Anita is an avid fan of exercising. Her father had taught her that exercise brought health to the mind, soul, and body. For Anita, exercise was one of the best ways to stay in tip-top shape and excellent health. She had seen the health club's ad for employment and applied. It would be a win-win situation. She could teach others to exercise, better their health, and be paid for it! Anita was brought on as an assistant manager and within ten days promoted to manager. She wore many hats under this title. She was a receptionist, exercise instructor, and salesperson. Upon returning a few years later she was brought on as manager and she still wore the same hats and more. This time, though, she could commit to it as a full-time career. She worked hard and earned good money. She had a plan of action! She would hold exercise classes when the other instructor would not or could not. The samurai was coming into play, again. A samurai's responsibility is to be of service to people. To the other instructors, holding the exercise classes was just a job. To Anita, it was a way of educating the clients to good health. Anita would sometimes hold as many as nine classes a day. The classes were filled with smiles and sweat! The clients walked away exhausted and energized! And they returned again and again for more! Anita got to know her clients very well. When it came time to renew memberships, dear Anita would reach out to them and make them the best offers available and they would accept and sometimes even enroll their friend(s).

Anita had savvy when it came to the health clubs. A savvy that caught the owner's eye. Anita would now begin to open the new clubs. Which was challenging, at first. You see, the owner would run ads promoting the opening of a club, and yet the club was not under construction (only an empty warehouse building). The ads would promote swimming pools, saunas, exercise rooms, weights, various exercise equipment, and nutritional supplements. It was Anita's job to sell the place, as is, to the prospective members. So, at first, Anita would show the empty warehouse to the clients, telling them that this was where the pool would be. And this was where the free weights would be. Over there was where the yoga room would be. After a few days, she talked with the potential clients and would point and say, "This is the pool, this is the sauna, and this is the yoga room." Anita visualized the completion of the club in her mind and carried it over to the clients' minds to see as well. And they saw in their mind's eye the beauty of the soon-to-be health club! When the club opened, Anita brought in the notion of babysitting for the clients. This allowed them freedom and more time at the club. It also allowed the women to have a break from being a mommy. They could have some "me" time. Now with laughter, I tell you that some of the women wanted a little bit more "me" time than they could find within the walls of the club. They would leave their youngsters at the club and disappear for shopping or lunch, or go to the hairdresser. Babysitting at the health club was free and empowering in more ways than one to clients! Anita's mother, Angelina, loves babies and children. Anita asked her to be the head babysitter to which she quickly agreed. She took care of all the children (which could be as many as thirty). She could hug, bounce them on her knee, feed, rock them to sleep, and play games with them and never tire. Now do you understand how Anita earned such good money? She had self-trust, could envision the possibilities around her, and had the clients' best interest in her mind and heart. She was being of service to and honoring them. The complete opposite of the owner's take of the business. Lucille was a very smart businesswoman regarding how to make money and have the clubs grow and spread out citywide, but she was neglectful of having empathy and concern for the clientele and employees. In short, to her, money came first, keeping money came second, clientele came third (because they paid her membership fees), and employees came last (provided they brought in revenue). If an employee did not bring in revenue, they were quickly out the door. Very cut and dry. Very cutthroat. A compassionate warrior such as dear Anita, though, can look beyond such an entity and move through and beyond them to ensure the betterment for all concerned.

During this time, while at the health center, Anita went back to school, part time. She went to community college. At first, she was not too sure what her education future held, but she knew that education held a key to her future. She began pursuing a degree in psychology. During this time, Anita also studied and became a certified exercise instructor. Sometimes you have to unlock many doors to find the correct door for your life's path. Please keep in mind, though, that there are no wrong doors, because even if the door may not be the correct door, at the moment, it does hold a life lesson for you in the future.

And this was the case regarding community college. She was learning and getting excellent grades, but was not moving forward in a manner that would promote growth regarding her career. While at the health club, she realized that she had what it took, physically, to open and run clubs, such as the ones she was promoting and working. Anita realized that she needed to go to another school, so she may have the "pen and paper" knowledge needed to successfully run her own business. She transferred her credits from the community college to Stony Brook University with the vision to obtain a degree in economics.

While studying at Stony Brook University and working at the health club, Anita's main focus was on her career and moving forward with success, for herself and others who played a role in her life. Anita was advised by one of her most trusted professors that, if she really wanted to be successful regarding her career, she needed to quit work and go to school full time. Anita, being a dragon of quick thinking, self-assessment, and fierce determination, agreed that this must be her next plan of action. Dear Anita was about to take flight into a new world where the open sky would take wing with boundless possibilities!

Chapter 7

Flying Anita

Freedom in the Sky

A new world of freedom to studying full time was opening for dear Anita. First, she did give her notice to Lucille at the health club. True to form, Lucille did not care that Anita, the person, left. Lucille's only concerns were that she was losing a money-maker and how was she going to get another employee to work that hard and bring in that much money. Not Anita's concern, though. She had given her very best to Lucille, the company, and the club members while employed, and now it was time to soar to new horizons. Anita now had the freedom to go to school full time. A full-time student she became at Stony Brook University (which was an hour's drive from home) who would later graduate with Phi Beta Kappa honors. Funny story about the Phi Beta Kappa. Anita received the letter from the Phi Beta Kappa Association and thought they were a sorority. She was about to throw it away because she was not one to partake in campus activities due to time constraints when her friend stopped her and insisted that she open it. Anita discovered that it was an honor, not readily given, to be a part of the Phi Beta Kappa. To qualify, a student needed to have excelled in Math, Science, English, and a foreign language. With English being her second language, Anita felt a little less than with her vocabulary and writing skills. No more, though, because she then realized that she was not alone when it came to mastering vocabulary and writing. Another freedom for her!

Also, the professor who had advised Anita to go back to school full time suggested that she become a part of the Victim Witness Research Program that was located in Brooklyn (two and a half hours, one way, from Stony Brook University). Anita would drive up to seven hours a day commuting from home to Stony Brook University, after classes to Brooklyn and then back home. The Victim Witness Research program was not a well-paying job, but what it did give her was priceless law experience to put in her mind and on her resume. Law school had gently fallen on to her pathway and she was seeing the future road toward it. Meanwhile, she was still following the road to the airport to watch the planes take off and land. One Saturday morning, parked at the airport, prior to Anita graduating with Phi Beta Kappa honors from Stoney Brook University, she decided then and there that she was going to learn how to fly. Period. Now keep in mind, my dear Anita had already learned to fly a tricycle, but now that she was older, she was ready to fly a bigger aircraft—a single-engine Cessna plane!

Anita went to three commercial flying schools. At each school, she sat and observed how the students were being trained and each time she was offered a ride for $50. She was not impressed by the feeling she got from these schools and left. Finally, at the fourth flying school, she met Mr. D'Angelone. At the school, which was in a hangar at the airport, he was sitting with two other seasoned pilots telling a story, saying, "…there I was inverted and on fire…" Anita knew she was at the right place! She asked him if she could go on the $50 ride that she had heard so much about. He responded in a no-nonsense, why are you bothering me, Italian accent, "Look, lady, this is a school and we don't do rides. Besides, keep your money and go home. You will never finish the program and get your license." The dragon in Anita was saying to herself, "Oh no, you don't make the rules for me," and the warrior was saying, "These are fighting words!" Anita replied in a compassionate warrior, insistent tone, "I am going to fly, and here is my money." To which Mr. D'Angelone replied, "Okay, let's go!" Dear Anita's heart beat with excitement to be in the sky!

Mr. D'Angelone proved to be a bit of a dragon himself at first. One of the stereotyped dragons that breathe fire and like to cause mayhem. He walked Anita to the little yellow two-seater plane and told her to get in on the left-hand side (the pilot side) as he climbed in on the right. He sat in the passenger seat with his arms crossed with no intention of flying. He blazed his words of flying instructions to her at lightning speed. "You see that white line? Keep the plane going straight with these pedals on the floor and push that red button. Pull the yoke, the wheel, back firmly, but steadily." He finished with, "You said you wanted to fly. Fly!" The warrior in Anita was determined to fly and the dragon was ready for an adventure. Her courage and self-trust were present and accounted for. Dear Anita looked at Mr. D'Angelone and saw that he didn't look suicidal, so she followed his instructions as he continued to sit cross-armed, and down the runway, they went and up into the sky they began to fly. A little wobbly at first, but nonetheless, successfully in the air taking flight. After many years, Anita Aiki Dragon was, once again, feeling the exhilaration and empowerment of being in the sky and flying. Her childhood innocence was alive, smiling with freedom and glee as she soared the cloud-filled heavens. It was at this moment that her inner spirit stated, "If you start something you must finish it." Just like the movement of the plane, that inner spirit thought glided from her mind to her heart and took flight in all ventures moving forward.

Another door had just been ajarred and Anita was going to open it full throttle and enjoy the independence of being a young woman flying in an age-old world being seen with new eyes!

Mr. D'Angelone was a really good guy! We dragons like to see into words and if you look closely at the name "D'Angelone" you will find the word "angel." That truly is what he proved to be for Anita. He was a guardian angel in the sky for her. He made their flying experiences fun and purposely challenging. A warrior loves challenges! If you look up the word "blast," one of its definitions is "a strong gust of wind." And that's what dear Anita was in the sky! She was a blast! Furthermore, I tell you, as I chuckle, she had a blast being a blast! She welcomed Mr. D'Angelone's challenges. His challenges were a form of protection for Anita. He would give her emergency situations and leave it to her to problem solve the urgency on hand. One time, while in the sky, Mr. D'Angelone distracted her and cut the engine and said to her, "What are you going to do now?" Her first thought was not of despair, but that there must be a place to land. Sure enough, in front of her materialized a small strip of land and she landed the plane. Of course, the landing was much different from that of a smoothly paved airport runway! Nonetheless, a safe landing had been successfully performed. Just what the emergency had called for! Once when Anita was concentrating on landing, following a large jet plane and talking jargon to the tower, Mr. D'Angelone opened the passenger door, leaned over, and started barking like a dog. The plane began tilting to the passenger side. Anita had to, quickly and with automatic reflexes, adjust the plane back to being level so they could continue flying the correct landing pattern. Safely to the ground they landed. It kind of sounds like Mr. D'Angelone was being mean to Anita, doesn't it, but he was not. He loved her as if she was one of his own children and he wanted to make sure that she was a safe pilot and could handle any flying emergency.

In one of their flying lessons, he instructed dear Anita to go high into the sky. Which she did. Suddenly, he told her to lift the nose of the plane too high. Which she did. This caused the plane to lose lift and stall. He then jammed the rudder to one side. The plane was now spinning downward from the sky to the earth. Fast! Fast! Fast! The plane was spinning over and over in a downward spiral. Anita, in her mind, was facing death. She experienced no dizziness and was totally aware of what was taking place. In the background, Mr. D'Angelone calmly stated to her, "Let go of the yoke. Now firmly, yet slowly, pull back on the yoke. If you pull back too quickly, the wings will rip off. Bring the yoke, s-l-o-w-l-y, to your abdomen." Which she did. The plane gradually began to fly straight and level as it should. You see, Mr. D'Angelone's course of spinning was a gift of love to dear Anita. This form of training was no longer required by the FAA (Federal Aviation Administration), but he wanted her to be aware of the experience, just in case. This was a very good thing, because one afternoon, while in flight by herself, she saw her university and leaned slightly to the left, causing the plane to stall and spin downward. She recalled the calmness of Mr. D'Angelone's voice saying, "Let go of the yoke. Now firmly, but slowly, pull back on the yoke" and in a moment's movement, she was flying level again. Thank you, Mr. D'Angelone, for making dear Anita a safe pilot!

Another time, Mr. D'Angelone took Anita on a nighttime flight across the Long Island Sound (an estuary of the Atlantic Ocean that lies predominately between Connecticut and Long Island) to experience vertigo. Once up in the sky, over dark water and under the night sky, Mr. D'Angelone had Anita cover her head with a hood and he did some shifting of the plane's flight pattern. Upon removal of the hood, it was Anita's responsibility to decipher what was going on with the plane. Was it still on course to the correct destination? Was it flying level? Was it inverted? At first, as was to be expected, dear Anita could not tell the plane's status. You see, vertigo is not the same in the air as it is on the ground. On the ground, you have a solid connection to the earth with your body. Once up in the sky, you lose that connection. You are no longer on earth. You are still of the earth, but your land becomes the moving plane within the sky; thus your equilibrium is based on the small flying world that has been created. The dark water and sky look and feel exactly the same to your body. Thus, you must let go of your personal senses and trust in the plane's instruments. You must connect full-heartedly with the plane's body and mind to ensure safety. Anita did just this. She reviewed and studied the plane's instruments. She could no longer rely on the Visual Flight Rules (VFR), where by her eyes she could fly; instead, she needed to focus on the Instrument Flight Rules (IFR). Her eyes needed to not be looking at the sky but to the plane's flight instruments. She put her trust in the flight instruments and responded to the information they were presenting to her. Swiftly and soundly she put the plane back on course for a safe journey back to home. A beautiful dragon always flies smoothly across purple waters and golden stars when her eyes are open to trust and oneness toward a constantly moving world that responds by encircling her in love and safety.

Mr. D'Angelone taught Anita a phrase she never forgot—"Flying is stretches of long boredom interspersed with moments of terror." And he gave her proof of it by the sudden emergencies that he created in the sky. This phrase allowed her, like with her car, to become one with the plane and fly the heavens. Flying was hard work, but she found peace in the seriousness and tension of it by remaining focused and at one with the plane and the sky, for that matter. Flying proved to be another form of meditation where she could receive complete freedom and joyfulness. She loved flying alone and having her own space to explore. To be so high and see all the communities, homes, roadways, waterways, and ant-sized people! Flying helped to put things in a bird's-eye view, for dear Anita, and to realize what seemed like a big problem was not. She acquired the perspective of universality. That everything whether it be a human, dog, ferret, deer, house, brick, tree, dragon, grain of sand, wheat field, or energy of any kind is all part of the creation and life of the universe.

Also, just so you are aware, there is a lot more to flying than just flying. There is the groundwork that needs to be done. Prior to taking off and after landing, a safe pilot must ensure that their plane is safe; therefore, they do a checklist of the plane. This checklist includes walking around the plane checking the fuel and oil levels, removal of the chocks, checking tires and brakes, checking the nose, inspecting the propeller and spinner for any possible damages or dents, checking the exhaust, and inspecting the tightness of the cowling screws. Anita enjoyed this routine of checking the safety of the plane to the extent that she became a ground instructor for other students. She taught them not only how to inspect the planes, but educated them on the science of flight, weather conditions, contact with the tower, and the mechanics of the engine. Also, this was dear Anita's way to prove to Mr. D'Angelone that she was serious about flying and was going to succeed in her pilot license.

Mr. D'Angelone signed her off to take the FAA exam (which he gave as an FAA examiner) after she met his personal criteria of what it takes to be a safe pilot. His criteria were simple and to the heart—"I will sign you off if I trust you to fly my children." Dear Anita had earned his trust. Anita did receive her flying license! There was a tradition that the school used to do with new pilots and that was to cut off their ties and post them to the wall of the flight school. Anita was the first female to graduate and did not wear ties; therefore, a new tradition of cutting off the back of a shirt was created. Anita had prior knowledge of this tradition and nearing graduation, she wasn't too sure when they'd be cutting the back of her shirt, so she got into the habit of always wearing a leotard under her shirt. She was a safe pilot with a safe plane and a safe body! Her shirt hangs on the wall of the flight school amongst all the men's cut ties. FYI, while at Stony Brook, Anita started her own flying club. As president, vice president, and secretary, she was able to successfully run the club and recruit members. Off into the sky those brave souls flew! Well, there was one semi-brave soul too. Anita took her good friend Bruce up in the air one early Saturday morning and everything was going fine. Both were laughing and joking and enjoying the sky and the view of familiar places that covered the ground. After about an hour of sightseeing, it was time to return to the airport and land. Upon getting close to the airport, Anita reached for the flight guide book, and she noticed that Bruce suddenly was no longer laughing. You see, he mistook the flight guide book for the landing manual. He suddenly began to panic, because in his mind Anita was looking at instructions on how to land the plane. In reality, though, she was looking for the radio frequency needed to make contact with the tower. Also, due to the crosswinds, Anita needed to make the landing at an angle, so now it appeared to Bruce that she would be missing the runway. Bruce began to panic and scream. Anita was aware that in his panic he may try to grab the yoke to prevent what he was thinking may be an inevitable crash. Anita was thinking she may need to use the fire extinguisher, near her, to knock him out to keep them safe. Alas, though, a few quick and loud shouts of "quiet" brought him back to his senses and a successful landing was performed!

Lastly, another part of flying that dear Anita really enjoyed was talking to others on the plane radio. Dear shy Anita! Uh-huh! Anyway, once when landing at John F. Kennedy International Airport, one of the busiest airports in the United States, where clearance for landing can take a great deal of time, she lowered her voice in a playful, alluring tone when talking to the tower because the male pilots were radioing in and speaking over one another in hopes of getting the first clearance to land. Tower control instructed all the other pilots to please be quiet and let the lady speak. Anita began to speak clearly and kindly and received immediate clearance for landing. After which, she said quietly to herself, "It's good to be the queen." Little did she know, at the time, that she was the queen. Dear Anita Aiki Dragon, in a few years, would discover that she was destined to become the Dragon Queen.

Chapter 8

Evolving Anita

Trust the Universe Is Always Working for Your Higher Good

Law School? Really? That was the thought that first breathed into dear Anita's mind when a friend of her father suggested that Anita go to law school. Yet, with the exhalation of the same breath, she realized that the answer was yes. Law school was where she was meant to be. A successful career could be made as a lawyer and, most importantly, she could be of service to others in need. Dear Anita's life up to this point had taken a journey on many roads to include the support and protection of loving parents, travels, employment loves, the revealing ways of people, education, friendships, and celebrations. All these roads had led dear Anita, the compassionate warrior, to the present path of wisdom. Anita was becoming a wise, compassionate warrior filled with more love and gratitude for all that was surrounding her. Anita knew that law went hand in hand with truth and justice. Anita's father, as you remember, lived a life filled with a strong emphasis on truth, justice, and principles. Dear Anita felt his empowerment within herself as well, and moved forward with the quest of completing law school and becoming a lawyer.

Through her professor, Anita had already begun the Victim Witness Research Program, which was an asset in her getting into law school. Anita also studied for and took the LSAT and passed with flying colors! She applied at several schools including Hofstra University. Anita's merit of being a Latino woman warranted that Affirmative Action be synchronized in her acceptance into Hofstra University's Juris Doctor Program. She and two other individuals (for a total of two female Cubans and one male Puerto Rican) had entered Hofstra University that semester with the assistance of the Affirmative Action Program. With the acknowledgment of having been accepted into law school, Anita asked her parents if she could return home to live, and with open arms, they lovingly said yes. Love and gratitude flourished!

About a month before law school was to begin, Hofstra University sent to Anita a work packet instructing her to write a brief based upon its enclosed legal information and the law to which it applied. Jokingly, Anita would say that she didn't know what a brief was except for men's underwear! Dear, dear Anita! You always find a way to make me smile! She did excellent with writing her brief and having it ready for the first day of class. Dear Anita sometimes finds writing to be challenging, but that's okay because it makes the warrior come out and work with tenacity! With very little sleep, a lot of perseverance, and an abundance of pure energy, she was able to complete her brief and stand with pride when turning it into the professor. Excellent, my dear Anita, excellent!

During the first day of school, Anita was standing in line, making photocopies of her work, and she had, if you will, a Yin and Yang moment. She turned her head back and saw two young men near her. One was a taller guy with a badly burned face who was obnoxious and fresh (and not in the sense of clean towels fresh, but of a sexually demeaning manner) toward Anita, and the other was a paraplegic man, confined to a wheelchair, with the face of a cherub, who treated

Anita kindly and with politeness. Needless to say, Anita had nothing further to do with guy number one, and with guy number two she commenced with a friendship of mutual respect and trust. Anita saw those two guys from their inner selves and not their outer selves. She knew the difference between off-putting darkness and inviting light. As always, Anita welcomed the light into her world! This light's name was Kenneth. He was a gift from heaven!

Most of the students at Hofstra University were from strong academic backgrounds and had known from an early age, primarily from their lawyer parents, that law school was to be in their future. Anita, although she had said yes to law school and was very grateful for the opportunity to be a lawyer, did not really want to be in law school. In short, she wanted out. Don't confuse out with quit. No, Anita did not want to quit, but she did want to receive her degree, as soon as possible. She committed herself to a plan of two years. She would go to school nonstop, which meant not only no summer or winter breaks but no internships, either. Her advisors emphasized to her that this would be a big mistake and that she needed to intern with top, well-known law firms for the experience and to get a future job with them. Dear Anita, the self-trusting warrior, charged forward leading her own path.

Law school proved to be very demanding both physically and mentally. Law professors did not always talk with politeness in their voices. On the first day of school, one of Anita's professors said to the students, "Look to your right; look to your left. One of you will not be here." In doing as such, the professor reinforced to them that at the least, one of the three would not last long enough for graduation. No worries, though, from Anita. After dealing with flying she knew she couldn't get killed in here! The professors also tried to belittle and put doubt in the students' minds. Students would come to class prepared to discuss their briefs and the professors would only find fault. Keep in mind that this fault was through the professor's perception of how they wanted it to be and not necessarily the way it truly was. A person's perception can be a gift or a theft to another person or even to themselves, depending on their intent. Dear Anita was aware of this and never lost sight of her own self-trust. She knew there was no room or need for self-doubt. Anita persevered with her own perception of what was and what wasn't. It never faulted or failed her. A warrior's mind always stays focused and at one with the truth.

Not only were there classes to attend, which Anita had to prepare for prior to attending, but consistently and constantly tests were needed to be taken and briefs to be written. Anita studied day and night. Even in her sleep she studied. Anita taped her voice onto cassettes and played them as she was falling asleep and again in the morning as she was waking. This made a big difference in her learning and retaining the information and being prepared for her tests. The briefs she wrote had to be laboriously detailed as to how she was going to present her case, including usage and definition of the law as to how it pertained to the case, the points she was going to stress, and the conclusion needed to win the case. Plus, there were mock trials and state competitions that she had to prepare for and participate in. Her friend Kenneth was in one of the trials. She did not know he was the one she'd be opposing, and her strategy for a win was not one that could be used successfully toward a paraplegic individual. On the spot, during the trial, she had to rethink and formulate a new tactic. As a quick thinker and talker, Anita was able to proceed in winning the case.

Sometimes, dear Anita just used her wits and sense of humor when dealing with professors. Especially Professor Friedman. He was one who ruled his class with an iron fist. He was not the most upbeat of personalities. He had a habit of putting his students down. His tests were hard. He was a famous trial lawyer, and his attitude was that the student was already a lawyer, and if you made a "C" on the test, then you made a good grade. This was somewhat worrisome to Anita because she needed an "A" in the class to remain in the top ten. Nothing was going to keep her from being in the top ten. Dr. Friedman did have one redeeming policy in his classroom and that was he liked people to raise their hands when he asked questions. He would give extra credit toward the test. Anita was always ready with her hand up and she answered his questions with eagerness and pride. Dr. Friedman, though, did not miss a chance to attack the argument of those who answered his questions, because he wanted to ensure they defended it! When students answered he would sometimes clip his nails or walk out of the classroom. He even told dear Anita that she was entitled to her own opinion no matter how wrong it was.

Finals time came and Anita had her choice of either taking a written or oral exam. She opted for the oral exam (and so did three other students) for she felt she would perform much better with an oral than a written exam. Dr. Friedman's final exam questions were in the back of his Contract textbook. At the time of the exam, Dr. Friedman would choose test questions for Anita to answer. There were a total of twenty questions. Anita studied and prepared herself to be ready to answer any question he may ask with the exception of one. This one question she quickly read and believed it to be more of criminal law (which the professor was to teach the next semester) than of contract law, thus it did not really belong with the questions to be answered. Guess which question Dr. Friedman chose? Yes, that's right. The question Anita had not prepared herself to answer. On his stand-up desk, he gave her the question, blank paper, and five minutes to write notes, so she would be prepared and organized in verbally answering the question. She stared at the paper in disbelief. Dear Anita could not make notes because she had not prepared for this question. She did not know the information needed to answer the question. When her five minutes were up, since she did not know the answer, she just started talking about sanctions. Dr. Friedman abruptly interrupted Anita by saying, "Ms. Arango, this is contract law, not criminal law!" Anita quickly and boisterously answered, "I know!" Dr. Friedman's prompting statement made dear Anita become so exasperated that she proceeded to explain to him why one could not have sanctions in contract law and that there can be no penalizations. Dear Anita, never at a loss for words or energy, continued answering the question with pure enthusiasm (not so much on the subject, but on the strong determination to make a high grade in the class). She made a "B" on the test! With the classroom extra credit, she made an "A" for the class and remained in the top ten!

As if there were not already enough demands in law school, Anita's Evidence professor gave his approval for her to be a part of his Trial Advocacy Program. This program would give Anita the opportunity to represent those individuals who had committed minor offenses, such as stealing beer. Anita agreed to be a part of the Trial Advocacy Program because this would give her hands-on experience regarding trial proceedings. The first client she represented was a 6'4" man with long blonde hair and covered with tattoos. Always respectful of others, Anita helped this individual to succeed with his case. Dear Anita, as you know, has respect for herself, as well. She learned, at this time, from her self-respect that she did not want to be a criminal lawyer. She had no judgment toward the individuals she defended, but she was not in favor of having criminal energy surrounding her. She much preferred love and respect for the law energy to surround her. She wanted all that was of honor to encompass her world of law. Dear Anita, the warrior, wanted to be of service to those whose world of honesty, family, and hard work had been altered in a mournful manner due to unforeseen circumstances beyond their control. She remembered what had happened as a little girl when she and her parents returned to Cuba and all their belongings had been taken from them. She knew the pain of something precious being taken away. Anita was strong of mind and body and had the never-ending energy to help those who needed compassion, kindness, protection, and the services of a resolute personal injury trial lawyer who was preparing to go to battle for their honor in the near future.

As you can imagine, law school was filled with stress and long hours of studying, preparing, and presenting. Saturdays proved to be wonderful days for Anita. On Saturday mornings, she would go flying and temporarily let the skies take over her mind and give her freedom from her earthbound tasks and responsibilities. Saturdays were also the day that she would be the ground instructor for the new students. She accepted no money for this job, but she was allowed to fly for free. For which she was very grateful. As you know, Anita is one to share her love, kindness, and knowledge with others. It was great fun for her to teach the students and to see their faces and reactions when she discussed why each of the tasks on the plane checklist needed to be completed and ensured for accuracy. Dear Anita wanted these aspiring pilots to become and remain safe pilots, as she had, and for them to enjoy a long lifetime of successful take-offs, landings, and fun-filled flights! The dragon in her wanted to hear their laughter resonate through the skies!

Saturday nights were meant for going out to dinner with friends. Relaxation, dinner, dancing, and being away from studying were her main priorities on Saturday night. Another Yin and Yang moment here! When Anita studied, she studied and there was no time for play. When Anita played, she played and there was no time for work. There must be a balance between work and play!

Sunday afternoons were great fun too. During summertime, she would drive down Jones Beach with the car music playing louder than the ocean waves and move to the rhythm. That got her warmed up for the actual dancing that was held every Sunday afternoon on Jones Beach. Dear Anita would dance all afternoon to all the different music. The dancing, wind, sand, sun, and being with people was the true definition of playtime to Anita. Cha-cha-cha! Alas, though, she knew playtime must come to an end until next week. By early Sunday evening, she was back home and studying for Monday's class and the week's timeline assignments.

Anita's really close friend at Hofstra University was Kenneth. He was a young man whose light shined with kindness and generosity. True he was paraplegic, and Anita had never had a physically disabled friend, yet he was like Anita in the sense that he had not only kindness and generosity, but a great mind and a willingness to share his knowledge for the betterment of others. He had his undergraduate degree in personal rehabilitation and was an expert when creating resumes. When dear Anita first talked with him alone, while they were on the elevator, she noticed that he had what looked to be a new wheelchair. She asked him if it was new. He lit up and said yes and then he went enthusiastically into detail discussing his wheelchair. It was then and there they became the best of friends. Many times due to illness caused by the confinement of the wheelchair, Kenneth missed class. No worries, though, because Anita never missed a class and at the end of the day she would take her notes to him so he could study and succeed in school. Later, during Anita's last semester of law school, one of her fellow classmates had received a "thank you, but no thank you" letter from a top law firm in New York City, and showed it to her. It stated that he had all the qualities needed for the position except for one, being a pilot. Anita realized that she had all the qualities needed, including that of being a pilot. Her energy was spinning and she was ready to apply and be hired! The only thing she needed was a resume. Kenneth makes his entrance. As an expert in resume writing, he took Anita's life and work experiences and made for her an absorbing, riveting, and commanding resume that eventually would fall into the hands and be read by the owner of one of the United States and United Kingdom's most respected law firms. Where kindness and generosity are shared by two close friends, anything is possible. Add the unconditional willingness to share your knowledge for the betterment of another and the universe smiles in harmony. Gratitude, love, and kindness is the way of the wise, compassionate warrior.

Chapter 9

Attorney Anita

Synchrodestiny and the Lucky Dragon

Not too long ago, my dear Anita said to me, "My life is like dragon sprinkles of good luck! I have lucky days. Whatever happens is lucky. Even if bad should happen it's lucky because it gives me something to study." So true, my sweet Anita Aiki Dragon. So true! She knows her Yin and Yang so well! I am eternally full of pride when I think of Anita's way of the world. She gently caresses all of life's elements and beings with the warm, harmonious energy of her hands and heart. She generously shares her dragon sprinkles with others as you will soon see.

Do you remember the Pan Am Building where Anita went to apply for a position as a flight attendant? And remember she did not get the position? That was a lucky day where something bad happened. Thus she studied and reflected and surmised it simply was not meant for her to be a flight attendant. Yet, within a few days, a lucky day came that was filled with good. That was the day when she was introduced to law school. As you know, she did excellent in law school and graduated with summa cum laude honors. Another lucky day came a few days after she had submitted her resume, which was created by her dear friend Kenneth, to the aviation law firm Speiser Krause. On that lucky day, they called her requesting that she interview with them. Guess where their office was located? The Pan Am building!

Dear Anita could not wait for the interview! Anita's excitement and buoyant energy were soaring high into the air! With the mind of a well-educated woman and the sparkling heart of a young girl, Anita got off the elevator on the 50th floor of the Pan Am building and entered the offices of Speiser Krause. She was greeted by a friendly man named Larry who introduced her to Mr. Krause. Mr. Krause was the managing partner of the law firm. All the attorneys were pilots and their main objective was to be a plaintiff's advocate in aviation or other mass disaster negligence. Their success in winning cases for their clients was due to extraordinary legal and technical knowledge and a solid commitment to being of service. Mr. Krause was a man with humor and great people skills. At their first meeting, he made Anita feel at home and gave her a tour of the law firm. Along the way, she met Mr. Speiser, a conservative man who was the founding owner and author of the firm, and Mr. Granito, a trial lawyer whose people's skills were not always present. During the interview, it was Mr. Granito who made the comment that Anita did not belong there. He stated aviation law was no place for emotional women. If you had been able to see Mr. Granito's manner of yelling his words in such an excitable and escalating tone, you would be thinking to yourself, did he say it was women who were emotional or men? Anita, knowing the compassionate warrior inside of her, knew instinctually to smile with warmth in her heart in the face of an attacker. Calmly she told Mr. Granito that he would not have those concerns with her. During the interviewing session, she simply smiled, showed the utmost exuberance, and answered all the questions with delight and enthusiasm. Anita wanted this job and what better way to show proof of wanting the job than to share an interest in the company and its clients. She asked questions of her own, which they respectfully answered. Dear Anita even asked, "How much vacation time do I get?" Mr. Krause, in a kind business voice, informed her that this type of question is not one that should be asked during an interview. Anita, not being disrespectful or crass, went into a dissertation explaining the reasons why vacation was very important to one's well-being. Dear Anita was ready to be of service, yet she knew that there needed to be a balance between work and personal life as well.

Toward the close of the interview, Mr. Krause informed Anita that there was not a position currently open and she had been invited for an interview because they wanted to meet the person who had such an entrancing resume. Dear Anita was crushed, but with kindness in her heart, she thanked the gentlemen for their time and bid them a good farewell. In leaving the law firm and getting into her car, she could not stop the tears from coming. And they kept coming. She wanted to work for Speiser Krause and be of service to their clients. She knew in her heart that she was meant to be an aviation attorney. With her tears and an empowering stance of being an aviation attorney, she went to the gym to work out. Anita was never one to remain idle no matter what the circumstances. Movement is action moving forward to be with what will be. The universe responds to such movements. While at the gym, Mr. Krause called Anita's home and spoke with her mother. He stated that Anita was to report to Speiser Krause on the following Monday at 8:00 a.m., sharp! Movement in motion had just taken place for dear Anita.

So much has happened, thus far, in dear Anita's life. Many movements in motion have led up to this moment. Anita is beginning to understand how being in the right place at the right time can create the highest good for yourself and those around you. Anita is beginning to realize the enlightenment of synchrodestiny. Synchrodestiny is when events, thoughts, people, signs, and/or messages align with the path of your life's purpose. Synchrodestiny may be considered coincidences, but they are not accidental. They are loving gifts from the universe that connect to your life's flow and create empowerment for yourself and those around you. There are many fascinating examples of synchrodestiny that occurred for Anita prior to, during, and after law school. To begin, there was Anita's repetitive gesture of driving to the airport to watch the planes take off and land. This led to her wanting to be a flight attendant. After applying for the position at the Pan Am building, she was turned down. Synchrodestiny does not mean that we always get what we want at the given time. Sometimes, a want and a need can become befuddled with each other, and we have to be told "no" to our want so we can be told "yes" to our need. Being told "no" can cause us temporary sadness, but the "no" will prove to be beneficial for our future. Dear Anita's "no" turned to "yes" many times over. Yes to taking flight classes. Yes to becoming a pilot. Yes to law school. Yes to friendships, during law school, to Larry and Kenneth. Yes to a good rapport with her college professors. Flight school allowed Anita to become a pilot, which allowed her to become an aviation attorney. Law school allowed her a law education, which allowed her to become an aviation attorney. A good rapport with her college professors allowed her to join the Victim Witness Research Program, Trial Advocacy Program, and State Competition Trials, which allowed her law experience to be placed on her resume, which allowed her to become an aviation attorney. Anita's friendship with Larry, through his employment denial letter, allowed her dear friend Kenneth to create a resume, through his exceptional resume writing skills, which allowed Anita an interview with an aviation law firm (located in the Pan Am building), which allowed her to become an aviation attorney. Thus, being an aviation attorney to those whose universes had suffered unjustly from manmade negligence and chaos allowed dear Anita to be of service to others, which allowed for their empowerment and betterment. Synchrodestiny in full circle.

Now, let's proceed on with dear Anita's life as an aviation attorney with Speiser Krause, and as we go along we will discuss more synchrodestiny moments. Once she received the news to be at Speiser Krause the following Monday, Anita knew she wanted to look her very best. Of course, my dear Anita always looks her very best no matter the occasion. It is the dragon in her and a quality that she inherited from her father. He consistently dressed handsomely in three-piece suits. Style and beauty have always been a part of Anita's life. She spoke with her father regarding the necessity of business clothes and he generously gave her money to buy her attorney attire. Anita knew the clothes should be conservative, yet have a bit of flamboyancy to express herself. A dragon at heart! She decided on two business suits (jacket and skirt). One was a striking burgundy red and the other was a regal navy blue color (which had a flair skirt). For both suits, she chose high-collar lace blouses. Naturally, elegant shoes and handbags accompanied the outfits. Anita was exquisite in the style needed to be a successful aviation attorney. Beauty radiated from her mind, body, and soul. Her heart was opening its wings of love in preparation to soar the heavens to be of service to those in need.

Monday morning came and dear Anita was at Speiser Krause at 8:00 a.m. sharp! Sharp as in on time. Sharp as in style. Sharp as in mind. Not only was a new day unfolding, but so was a new world! A new world where a dragon can shine with her knowledge, splendor, and grace. A new world where a compassionate warrior can take a sword in hand and peacefully cut through chaos and despair to create a path toward honoring and healing soulful hearts and minds.

Anita's first day was a great first day! She had a little bit more interviewing to do and introductions to the attorneys she had missed in her previous interview. One of the attorneys she met was the one she was replacing. He had been terminated so she could be with the law firm. There were no hard feelings or unkindness toward Anita due to his termination. It was business as usual. Anita's spent a lot of the first day with Mr. Krause. He was explaining the ins and outs of the firm to include its history, the various cases they had successfully won, and what it means to be an active practice that goes to trial. He also discussed with Anita how impressive it was that she partook in the Victim Witness Research Program, Trial Advocacy Program, and State Competition Trials and how the experience would assist as a trial attorney with the law firm. As managing partner, Mr. Krause was the handler of all the trials. It was he who determined which cases would go to who. He had the utmost confidence in Anita. He did inform, though, that she needed to pass the bar, as soon as possible. Anita was aware of this and had already scheduled the bar exam and was in the process of studying and taking the class.

The class was intense. It lasted from 9:00 a.m. to 5:00 p.m. for two weeks. Each course was covered within ninety minutes followed by a ten-minute break. When it was time to take the bar exam (which lasted three days and had a passing rate of 40 percent), Anita stayed at the Barbizon Hotel (which when originally built was an all-woman's hotel whose guests included many notable names) to ensure less stress and more quality study time than that which could be found at the learning center. Anita was ready and full of confidence in taking the bar exam. Once completed, Anita smiled with triumph and happiness knowing inside herself that she had passed it. She never gave the bar exam a second thought. Not even while taking a bubble bath in celebration of a job well done! It would take the State Board of New York approximately three months to confirm what dear Anita already knew.

Almost immediately, Mr. Krause sent Anita to the National Transportation Safety Board (NTSB) hearings, in Boston, regarding the

Ocean Ranger Disaster. The NTSB is a U.S. government investigating agency that investigates various civil transportation accidents to include aviation, maritime, highway, pipeline, and railroad. Anita would soon play a very important role regarding the cases involving the *Ocean Ranger* Disaster, but for now, though, her main responsibility was to meet as many people as possible and return to New York with their business cards. Mr. Krause already saw how energetic and at ease Anita was toward people, so he knew she would do great in Boston. And great she did! She met and came back with most everyone's business card. A feat not easily done, but one that would prove very beneficial to Speiser Krause and the victims' family members. Anita never lost sight of her commitment to being of service to others, and she knew those business cards were more than someone's name on paper. Those business cards held the souls of the *Ocean Ranger's* victims, and their family members' fate lay innocently in her hands. A young dragon, in the water, has swum to the surface and sees what others have not. Love and protection are on the horizon.

Anita's first trial assignment, a gift from Mr. Speiser for having passed the bar, was a case that involved an airplane crash that happened three years earlier. Of all the attorneys she was to assist, it had to be Mr. Granito. Remember, he was the man who told Anita, in an excitable manner, that women were too emotional to be attorneys. He was so upset that Anita was assigned to him that down the halls of Speiser Krause, he was uncontrollably yelling over and over, "How could they give me such a neophyte to try the case!" Anita was mentally and physically ready to work with him. In fact, she had already prepared the brief and had handed it to him during his tirade. In his hand, without looking at it, he proclaimed that it was a piece of *sh*t* and that he was throwing it in the garbage. Which he proceeded to do. Dear Anita, without missing a beat, retrieved the brief and sent it on to the courthouse. Never tell a dragon something that isn't so because they know better. Anita knew her quality of work was more like a piece of *art!* She knew not everybody has an appreciation for art and that art can be seen differently between individuals. Also, she knew, when someone faulted art, it was usually because they did not understand the artist's intent to open one's mind and soul. No worries or judgment crossed Anita's mind, though. Just like she had educated Larry, from the park, on how wonderful Cubans were, Anita was going to educate, without punching him in the face, Mr. Granito on how wonderful an aviation attorney she was!

"Ms. Arango," groaned Mr. Granito, "your assignment is to leave on Friday for Niagara Falls and gather the witnesses from the plane crash and get them to agree to testify for Monday morning in court. Also, you need to find the courthouse, arrange all the court details, file the papers, and choose our seats. All this needs to be completed prior to my arrival on Sunday." Mr. Granito did not even have the courtesy to say thank you to dear Anita. With a smile, a beautiful smile, I must say, she thanked Mr. Granito and proceeded to make hotel and flight arrangements from New York to Niagara Falls. The kindness in my dear Anita's heart always showed in her smile! Anita, though not attached to, always had an appreciation for that which was first-rate; thus she booked first-class airline tickets and a stay at one of the better hotels in Niagara Falls. Dragons love all that is beautiful whether it be a tiny dragonfly hovering over a moss-covered stone or the sight of the sun illuminating the clouds from a plane's first-class passenger window. Anita knew once she landed in Niagara Falls, it was off to nonstop work. From the airport, she rented a car and began her trek of meeting with the witnesses and getting their agreements to testify on Monday. As soon as that was completed, she was off to accomplish all the assignments Mr. Granito had unsmilingly thrust upon her. Around midnight, with pride riding highly on her shoulders from a productive day of accomplishing her missions, Anita went to the hotel. She was envisioning her reward of relaxing with an order from room service and a warm bubble bath. Upon arriving, though, the hotel's concierge handed her eleven frantic messages from Mr. Granito requesting that she call him, ASAP. With a smile on her face Anita called Mr. Granito. He, on the other end of the phone, was not smiling and had a state of panic in his voice. "Ms. Arango," he yelled, "where have you been? I told Krause not to give me a neophyte and he wouldn't listen. He assured me that you knew how to get things done. We have court on Monday! Do you not understand the importance of your work?" With the gentleness of a mother bear rescuing her cub from a shallow stream, dear Anita serenely proceeded to tell Mr. Granito of her day's accomplishments and that everything was in place for Monday morning. After a long pause on Mr. Granito's end, he replied a quick "we'll see" and "good night." Still, no thank you. Anita hung up the phone with a gleam in her eye because she knew what had just taken place. Today had been another lucky day filled with opportunity regarding Mr. Granito. Anita picked up the phone, one more time, to call room service. She stated to room service, "Please send to my room steak and wine. Thank you." My dear Anita never forgot to say please or thank you to anyone. Gratitude is always present in those who embrace love in their heart. A few moments later she was drawing her bubble bath. Anita's day had been laboriously successful and she was going to enjoy the rest of her evening the way she had envisioned. Later, she would sleep with a peaceful mind and angelic smile while dreaming of the universe's beauty.

Monday morning came and Anita, true to her words to Mr. Granito, had everything lined up. Anita and Mr. Granito presented their case first to the judge. They worked well as a team, he as the first lead and she as the second chair. Their report of the accident and evidence of the burden of proof was so solid that the opposing team had no counterargument and tendered their policies. Anita and Mr.

Granito won the case! "Ms. Arango, thank you for all that you did to make today a success. I was wrong to have behaved the way I did in New York and over the phone. Again, I thank you," said Mr. Granito wholeheartedly. With a congratulatory handshake between them, Anita could feel in her hands Mr. Granito's energy of gratitude, sincerity, and appreciation. She could feel, too, the professional love and respect he had for her in his heart. She simply smiled more radiantly her beautiful smile. My dear Anita had just educated Mr. Granito to the fact that she was a successful aviation attorney.

A few hours later, over celebration drinks, Mr. Granito revealed to Anita he had once been a fighter pilot during the war. He shined brilliantly as he told her stories of his fighter flying days. While telling these stories his personality changed to being a man filled with the kind of euphoria that can only be in the freedoms and unexpected events that happen in the sky. Once he finished his stories, his personality returned to earth with his dream grounded. He knew what he needed to do to be successful as an attorney, but he did not know what to do to be successful as a man of a lost dream. Anita understood. Unbeknownst to him, she became a guardian angel to him. Silently, she sent him thoughts of love and encouragement for a world where he may have his dream. She helped him to smile through her smiles and laughter. In turn, Mr. Granito became Anita's protector. His heart continued to open and give knowledge lovingly to Anita. He always looked out for her best interest. He gave Anita the outstanding piece of attorney advice of "people will use you…be careful…all you have is your reputation." Dear Anita's reputation has always been one to hold honor in all decisions regarding the law and aspects of her life. A dragon would have it no other way.

Anita made it a point of working at the law the firm efficiently, enthusiastically, and fast! She achieved this by leaving the house at 4:30

a.m. to arrive early at the firm to begin her day. At lunch, she went to the gym for her daily workout. Upon returning from the gym, she would have a quick lunch while proceeding with the rest of her day's requirements. She would leave the law firm at 5:00 p.m. with Mr. Speiser (unlike other attorneys who would leave shortly after he left). Though not always predictable, Anita's days were precise and succinct in covering all requisites due to the fact that she could account for every minute of the day. Her lunch break workout was a godsend in more ways than one. First, it got her away from the law firm for an hour, thus allowing her to relax her mind and tighten the strengths of her physical self. Exercise has always been a key factor in Anita remaining in excellent health. So has the discipline of Chinese medicine, but we will discuss this later. Second, Anita met at the gym a most remarkable man, Allan, who was friendly, smart, funny, outgoing, and knew seven different languages. Most importantly he was a photographer with whom Anita would share a fascinating relationship. When they met, Allan was doing an article for *Time* magazine about executives who exercise during lunch. Allan interviewed her and took many photos of Anita's daily workout. Soon she was running weekly to the newsstand, just like a little girl running to see the circus, to ask the vendor if the new *Time* magazine was out. Weeks later, to the relief of the vendor, the edition, with Anita in it, arrived. My dear Anita was so excited and proud. With her childlike energy, she ran back to the law firm to show Mr. Speiser the article. "Mr. Speiser, Mr. Speiser, we are in *Time* magazine," Anita proclaimed as she jumped up and down in his office! Mr. Speiser was on the phone and told the person on the other end that he needed to hang up because one of his lawyers was jumping up and down in front of him. Mr. Speiser carefully removed his glasses, laid them on his desk, and asked her "What for?" He placed his glasses back on, gently smiled at Anita, and then proceeded to read the article. He put down the magazine, carefully put his glasses on the desk, and with a business-like smile stated to Anita, "The law firm was only mentioned once." Dear Anita, with the splendor of her excitement, informed Mr. Speiser that the next time she was in a magazine, she would see to it the company's name was mentioned many, many times! Mr. Speiser's gentle smile returned with a small chuckle and a big appreciation for Anita's cheerful sincerity.

Anita and Allan became close and shared fun times together. As a photographer, Allan always had passes to be on the sites of intriguing events and places. As Yin and Yang must coincide with each other, Allan would also be on the sites of horrific disasters. He would see those individuals whose worlds had been devastated due to tragedy. Generously and with permissibility within the law, he would enlighten them of Anita and how she could be of service to them. He would give them her business card and leave it up to them to decide if they needed her services. Allan was another aspect of how synchrodestiny played a role in Anita's life. Allan, through his magazine article, put Anita's pictures out into the world for all to see. With the pictures came her name and the name of the law firm for the world to read. Allan's generosity of releasing her business cards to those in distress allowed for direct contact with Anita. Allan brought to focus, similar to the way the lens of a camera catches the truth, the faithful authenticity of Anita's universal mission of being of service to those in need.

As a little time passed with the law firm, Anita realized that her workouts would work better in the mornings before beginning work. Primarily based upon using her time sensibly. She left home around 4:30 a.m. because if she left any later than that, it could change a forty-five-minute drive to almost two hours due to the traffic and toll roads. She presented to Mr. Krause her reasons for going to the gym before work and being at the law firm at 8:30 a.m. (instead of the usual starting time of 8:00 a.m.). He was understanding and in agreement. Dear Anita then had one more request of Mr. Krause. Due to her driving her car in every day, was it possible for her to have her own parking spot? It was not customary for an attorney to receive a paid parking spot due to the high cost of parking in New York; therefore, she gave him a dissertation as to why a parking spot for her was of such dire importance. Without a rebuttal, Mr. Krause granted her request. A dragon may use her words of honesty to justly earn an entitlement given to few. The universe will always open to those whose intent is to serve with honor.

A Mayday call was made from the *Ocean Ranger* at approximately 1:00 a.m. on February 15th indicating they had a major problem and needed immediate assistance. At approximately 1:30 a.m. the *Ocean Ranger* made one last transmission stating they were evacuating the platform and manning the lifeboats. In brief, the *Ocean Ranger* was, for its time, the largest semi-submersible offshore drilling vessel that was dubbed as being unsinkable. On February 6th, the Ocean Ranger had its first scare when the balance control began to unexplainably list. The weather conditions were good with a calm sea and the problem was solved. On February 14th, the date of dear Anita's birthday (synchrodestiny), a large storm hit the Grand Banks of Newfoundland, where the *Ocean Ranger* was stationed. The winds were as strong as ninety knots and the waves as high as fifty feet. At approximately 7:00 p.m. waves hit and broke the porthole window above the control system in the ballast control room. Saltwater hit and poured over the ballast control panel, causing it to short-circuit. The stability of the *Ocean Ranger* was at stake. The eighty-four-member crew did everything they knew to do to keep the vessel afloat and themselves alive. Unfortunately, due to the short-circuiting of the control panel, the listing of the vessel could not be permanently corrected. The listing became too severe. The crew attempted to launch the lifeboats, but the vessel continued to list, the strong winds blew stronger, and the sea rolled cold and rough; therefore, not all the lifeboats were put to use.

Some men in their last effort to live jumped off the vessel into the frigid waters, which caused their untimely deaths from hypothermia. Rescue vessels were attempting to assist, but due to the catastrophic weather conditions, rescues proved to be nonviable. At approximately 3:15 a.m. the *Ocean Ranger* sank. Neither vessel nor men survived. God bless those eighty-four men and their souls of courage.

Anita's heart beat with compassion and strength as she met with the fifteen lawyers who were representing the family members of the eighty-four *Ocean Ranger* losses. Her tone was solid with facts as she explained to the lawyers why she and the law firm should be the ones to represent the family members. Her words were generous with kind-heartedness as if she was actually speaking to the family members. Her eyes in looking at the print and photos of the *Ocean Ranger* disaster could see the savagery that had severed all chivalry. Benevolence breathed out through her eyes upon those images with the resolute determination of a courageous warrior to bring the resurrection of the lost souls back into the hearts and homes of their surviving families and loved ones. The agreements were made and dear Anita placed her feet securely on the ground and began her promise-filled warrior's walk across the land where the sun shines brightly, the wind blows peacefully, the trees are fruitful, and within viewing distance, the ocean waves roll harmoniously. The land where truths are found and souls dance in the rewards given by a grateful universe.

I must tell you of a humorous happening that took place with my dear Anita when she was first meeting with the fifteen lawyers. As she was greeting them she introduced herself by name only and not by title. The lawyers assumed that she was the secretary and started giving her coffee orders. Anita continued greeting them until they were seated at the large conference table. At that time, she sat at the head of the table and with a smile informed them that she was the Head of Damage

Control. The room became so silent that you could hear a pin drop in soft butter. Victory can take on many forms! Of course, thinking of Anita as a secretary was a stereotyping mistake, which was unlike the time the attorneys at her own law firm placed bets on how long she would last there. Most of the guys bet a month or less. Very insensitive of them. Did it bother Anita? No. Knowing Anita's sense of humor, she probably would have placed a bet on herself as well. The winning bet, that is, where she would be with the company as a successful aviation attorney for many, many years! Not only was she a successful aviation attorney, but she was the first female aviation attorney for Speiser Krause. Again, victory can take on many forms!

Anita had to take many steps while walking the warrior's walk when dealing with the *Ocean Ranger* Disaster case. First, she had to get the fifteen lawyers of the surviving family and loved ones to be in agreement for representation. Anita accomplished this almost immediately. Second, she had to meet with the judge to get state and federal jurisdiction and then file a case with the Federal Court. At the same time and continuously she had to do research and get all the information needed to present the case at trial and/or in litigation. Anita had to ensure that the information was accurate and truthful. There could be no fallacies. A reputation of honor and integrity must always shine above any darkness that may have fallen unjustly upon those being represented. Light attracts light. Truth will always be found in the light. What was discovered to have taken place during the *Ocean Ranger* Disaster were these truths.

The *Ocean Ranger* was notified early morning on February 14th that a cyclonic storm was forming and heading their way. At first, nothing was done regarding the protection of the vessel or crew. Like the *Titanic*, the *Ocean Ranger* had been categorized as unsinkable. Toward the end of the day, the vessel was taking necessary safety precautions, which included hanging off the drill pipe and disconnecting the drill riser. Communication between the *Ocean Ranger* and other nearby vessels remained open throughout the day and early evening with no signs of distress. At approximately 7:00 p.m. the *Ocean Ranger* transmitted that the porthole window above the control ballast room had been broken due to high waves and that saltwater had entered and saturated the control ballast system. The porthole was located only a few feet above the sea level (much lower than what it should have been, for it allowed more ocean water to come onto the vessel contributing to the sinking). At approximately 9:00 p.m. the *Ocean Ranger* communicated that the ballast control panel's valves were opening and closing on their own (which would allow water to come in and out and in turn would jeopardize the balance of the vessel). Unfortunately, the crew had not been trained on how to manually override the control system; therefore, they were at the mercy of a short-circuited instrument. Furthermore, the crew had not been thoroughly trained on how to man the lifeboats. Plus the lifeboats were not designed to be launched during rough seas. It was determined if the crew had been properly trained regarding the ballast control system and lifeboat safety procedures (to include functioning lifeboats for rough seas) that they would have survived.

The more dear Anita discovered regarding the events that took place on the final day of the *Ocean Ranger*, the more her heart cried for the souls of the crew. Dear Anita's tears were of the emotions of the crew's last few minutes to be alive. In her ears, she could hear their cries to the darkened sky for help and rescue. She could see the hope in their eyes as the lifeboats were initially being launched and attempted to be set to sea. She could feel their despair as the lifeboats fell clumsily off the launch tracks and into the sea half filled with men. She could feel their hope rise, again, when those in a successfully launched lifeboat were in reach of another vessel attempting to rescue them. With tear-filled eyes, dear Anita could see the lifeboat near the rescue vessel to which the men had tied their lifeline only for it to be severed by the strong ocean's waves. Anita could see the lifeboat turn over as the men reached upward in one final courageous attempt to grab the hands of the rescue ship's team. Anita's body could feel the icy cold water as the men fell into the sea for the last time. There was no moon nor stars that night. All was dark. The crew never got to see the next day's calm blue seas nor feel the warmth of the rising reddish-orange sun. Nor would they and their loved ones ever share the laughter, love, and dreams that once surrounded them all. Anita could feel the loved ones' torment.

A compassionate warrior will cry tears as they walk their path. They must. A warrior must feel the inner spirit of others so that they can be of honorable service to them. Once a warrior begins their journey they may only move forward. The tears, as they fall to the ground, create the reflections of what needs to be. Knowledge is found in tears. For three years, dear Anita's tears and heart gave her guidance as to what needed to be done for the loved ones of the *Ocean Ranger's* crew. Anita succeeded in creating victory for the crew and their loved ones. Although she could never return the crew's lives back to their loved ones, dear Anita's brave warrior's walk gave redemption to the crew's souls. The souls may return to the heavens knowing their loved one's lives were financially secure. Through Anita, the crew's souls were able to provide for the future of their loved ones. More importantly than money, dear Anita had given back the respect that had been cast away from the crew and their loved ones due to the neglect of the proper training needed for the crew to survive. Anita made the moon and the stars shine brightly once more over the waters from which life may come forth. So proud of my dear Anita I am. So very proud of my warrior I am!

My dear Anita can give me pride for her in more ways than one. Sometimes it can come by her sweet innocence of knowing that the truth must always fly high. Anita, as you know, was the first female aviation attorney for Speiser Krause; therefore, she was always surrounded by male attorneys. To balance all the maleness in the courtroom, Anita took great delight in being a woman and showing her feminine side. She proudly did this by wearing stylish hats and beautiful gold and diamond jewelry that her father had made for her. His love for her made Anita sparkle both of heart and attire! One day, in the courtroom, while in an attractive hat and wearing a gold airplane wing broach that her father had made, one of the defense attorneys made a request to the judge that Anita's hat needed to be removed within the courtroom. He further requested to the judge that she remove her airplane wings because he felt that Anita was trying to insinuate that she was an aviation expert. FYI, Anita never insinuates. There is no need for her to do as such. She does her homework and knows that which needs to be known. Period. Anita pointed out to the judge, through a written policy, that it was true that a man must remove his hat inside the courtroom, but a woman does not due to it being part of her attire. She also pointed out to the judge that the defense attorney was wearing a tie with airplanes, and his associate was wearing suspenders with airplanes. The judge was in favor of Anita, due to her facts being accurate and a fear of not having a fully clothed courtroom. Dear, dear Anita, you have always had a way of making the truth serve you well!

Another fashion distraction, if you will, was when Anita returned to St. John's to give the fifteen Canadian lawyers the settlement check for the *Ocean Ranger* Disaster case. She flew in the night before as to be rested and ready to go when meeting with the attorneys. At the airport, she could not find her luggage. She was informed the luggage was lost, but that they would work on locating it and send it on to her hotel. The following morning, there was no luggage to be found. She had two choices as to what she could wear to the meeting. Either her very casual flight clothes or her New Year's Eve outfit. Now, if you knew my dear Anita, as I do, the answer was very obvious! She chose the New Year's Eve outfit, which was a black spaghetti strap jumpsuit, stiletto heels, a small fur coat, and lots of gold and diamond jewelry (that her father made). Needless to say, it was an interesting and successful meeting! What a great way to start the New Year! My dear Anita has been the reason for much merriment in my heart and jubilation in my eyes. She is a precious jewel!

The New Year also brought a glorious love back, in person, to dear Anita. Her beloved Abuela Ana moved from Cuba to the United States! Everything fell into place for Abuela Ana's safe and swift move to New York. Within a month of having completed the paperwork on both the Cuban and American side, Abuela Ana and her husband, Pedro, were in the United States. Abuela Ana made it clear to Anita that she wanted her own place to live. Anita began the process of apartment searching. As good fortune would have it, Anita was able to find a newly renovated apartment complex in Queens for her grandparents. This was wonderful because it allowed Anita to visit her Abuela Ana every day! When she left work at 5:00 p.m. she would stop at Abuela Ana's on her way home. Her grandfather, Pedro, would stand on the top floor waving hello to Anita. Abuela Ana would embrace Anita with energies of love and protection. Abuela Ana was always wanting to keep Anita safe. Anita had been born with a "Don," which is a gift of being able to receive that which is needed. A gift of being a guide. Sometimes others can be jealous of such a gift and may try to harm. Abuela Ana was never going to let this happen. As a shaman, Abuela Ana had a ritual that she would perform on Anita. She would take an egg and pass it up, down, and all around Anita's body from the top of her head to the soles of her feet. Then she would spin Anita around three times, clockwise, raise her arms, and drop them to the floor. She would have Anita feel the egg for the negative energy that had been absorbed. The egg always felt heavier than it had prior to being passed over her. Once done, Abuela Ana would place the egg in a brown paper bag, with three dark pennies, and throw all later into the ocean. Then she would give Anita a B-12 shot for mental and physical strength and energy. Anita once told me that she could tell what kind of day her Abuela Ana had based upon the B-12 shot! On a good day, the injection went in smooth and on a not so good day, there may be more of a jab! As she told me this, Anita was laughing in great fondness and love for her Abuela Ana! Lastly, Abuela Ana would give Anita a strong cup of espresso. Simply because it is the Cuban thing to do! To this day, Anita still has one cup of espresso per day!

Wonderful Abuela Ana also helped Anita in her day-to-day life of dealing with other people. A few times during court she would reach out to Abuela Ana and ask her to sweeten a judge. Abuela Ana would write the judge's name on a piece of paper and place it in a jar of honey. The judge would sweeten up and rule in Anita's favor. Anita once told her grandmother of a coworker who was not a particularly kind person. Abuela Ana put their name in a jar of honey and within a few days they moved on to a better job with another company. Please be aware, as a shaman, Abuela Ana could do no harm or direct negative energy toward anyone. Through her power, though, of universal love, she could sweeten them with kindness so that they did not harm Anita. Abuela Ana was a remarkable woman and spirit!

During the three years of handling the *Ocean Ranger* Disaster case, my dear Anita, on a return flight back from an aviation and space law conference in Washington, D.C., met an extraordinary Japanese man. He spoke little English, but Anita knew enough Japanese to have a nice conversation with Mr. Tanaka during the flight. Mr. Tanaka was a gentleman in the truest meaning of the word. He was a gentle, courteous, and sincere individual who had great respect for others. Mr.

Tanaka could feel the tenderness and sincerity in Anita's voice and he knew, during that flight, that she was a woman of honesty. One of the topics of their discussion was the aviation and space law conference. You see, Mr. Tanaka was a media expert as a space program writer. He was the author of magazine articles, journals, and books. He politely asked Anita if she would please send him copies of the literature she had obtained at the conference. My dear Anita replied as she slightly bowed her head, "Hai, sore ga watashi no yorokobi desu" (Yes, it would be my pleasure). The following morning, Anita sent Mr. Tanaka the literature. A few days later, Mr. Tanaka replied to Anita with a beautiful thank you card, expressing in English and Japanese his gratitude and appreciation for her kindness.

Not too long after sending dear Anita the thank you card, Mr. Tanaka flew from Japan to New York, and upon his unannounced arrival at the law firm, he requested a private meeting with her. Anita was initially surprised to see Mr. Tanaka, yet it gave her joy to see the kind gentleman again. At the beginning of the meeting, Mr. Tanaka reminded Anita that when they parted from the Washington, D.C. flight, she had graciously told him to contact her if ever there was anything she could do for him. Anita remembered well. At the time she made the gesture, Anita thought he may reach out to her by phone or mail, if need be. It never occurred to her that he would make a personal flight of such great distance to see her. She was honored by his presence and ready to be of service. Mr. Tanaka, a very private man, expressed the sadness that had been in his heart for nearly twenty years. He and his wife had divorced many years ago. When the divorce became finalized, his wife took their two small children (a son and a daughter) and disappeared. Every day he missed his children more and more, but he had not reached out to them for two main reasons. First, his ex-wife had told the children, when they were very young, that he was dead. Second, he did not want to upset their innocent world. The children were now adults (eighteen and nineteen years old) and he felt this was the appropriate time to reach out to them. They, as adults, may make their own decisions as to whether or not they wished to have him enter back into their lives. Mr. Tanaka gently told Anita he knew from the way she had spoken her words on the plane that she held a noble heart that contained love's earnestness to seek out the truth, no matter what the outcome may be. He asked Anita to please help him find his children. The only information he had regarding his children was that their last name was Whitehead and that they lived in California. Anita asked Mr. Krause if she could use the law firm's investigative branch to search for Mr. Tanaka's children. Mr. Krause stated yes and that there would be no charge. Anita relayed the information to Mr. Tanaka. Mr. Tanaka thanked dear Anita with his words and joyful smile of immeasurable hope that shined from his face.

The Speiser Krause investigative branch began doing legal investigations in search of Mr. Tanaka's children. Within a month's time, they had located them. Anita first called the son and he was elated and instantly in agreement to meet his father. Anita next called the daughter and she was shocked, did not believe, and was resistant. Eventually, she understood and agreed to meet her father. Anita's heart beat strong of love. She knew she was opening the children up to their father's love. Through her father, she knew how beautiful and enriching a father's love was for his children. Anita contacted Mr. Tanaka to let him know the status. Dear Anita, in a loving voice, informed Mr. Tanaka that his children had been found and that their love for him was very much alive and that they wanted to meet with him. Dear Anita's two words, "children's love," released the sadness from his heart and filled it with happiness. Anita continued with more happy news. Mr. Tanaka's daughter was a full-time college student, and his son was enrolled in the space program to become an astronaut. Synchrodestiny in action— Mr. Tanaka as a space program writer and his son preparing to be an astronaut. His children had done well for themselves. This gave Mr. Tanaka great pride! He also had great pride and appreciation for Anita. She with the help of the investigative branch had reconnected him with his children for which he was eternally grateful. Can you begin to see the synchrodestiny being created between dear Anita and Mr. Tanaka?

"There must be a movie star or president around here," my dear Anita said to her mother as they got off the plane in Japan. Photographers were running to and fro, snapping pictures in her direction. Amongst the flashing of the bulbs, she saw Mr. Tanaka coming toward her. Each bowed while saying hello and wishing the other a good day. "Welcome to Japan, Ms. Arango," stated Mr. Tanaka, "and what do you think of your reception?"

"My reception?" questioned Anita.

"Yes! The reporters and photographers! They are here for you! An article is to be written in honor of your visit to Japan," proclaimed Mr. Tanaka.

My dear Anita, never shy of people or cameras, smiled gracefully with gratitude, and kindly replied, "My reception is beautiful. Thank you."

Mr. Tanaka, with the photographers in the background, proceeded to take Anita and her mother to the hotel where they could freshen up after their long flight. Anita and her mother stayed at the luxurious Prince Hotel in the center of Tokyo. The hotel was beautiful and set in a small forest of trees and greenery. While Anita's mother rested, Anita was going over her notes regarding the Korean Air Lines Flight 007. The flight had originally taken off from New York City, New York, and had a stopover in Anchorage, Alaska. After taking off from

Anchorage, while in flight for Seoul, South Korea, it flew through Soviet-prohibited airspace and was shot down by a Sukhoi Su-15 (a Soviet twinjet supersonic interceptor aircraft). Approximately fifteen minutes after the two missiles hit the plane, it crashed near Moneron Island in the Sea of Japan, killing all 246 passengers (which included twenty Japanese citizens) and twenty-three crew members. The Japanese are of a culture where integrity and honor are of the utmost importance in family life. Respect for all whether in life or death is held in high esteem. The president of Korean Airlines did not acknowledge the passing of the twenty Japanese citizens; therefore, the surviving family members were insulted by the lack of respect shown and chose to sue Korean Airlines. The warrior in Anita was taking her stance of readiness to be of service. A few days prior to arriving in Japan, Anita had reached out to Mr. Tanaka to see if he might be privy to the Japanese lawyers representing the surviving family members, so she may have the opportunity to interview with them concerning the representation of their clients. Mr. Tanaka remembered the kindness Anita had shown in locating his children and informed her that he would make the meeting happen and for her, and her mother, to be his guests in Japan. Mr. Tanaka had great admiration for Anita. He affectionately held her close to his heart with feelings of love and respect. With Anita, he had a loving friendship of spirit. He was pleased that she had made it safely to Japan.

Later that evening, over dinner, which included dear Anita's first taste of sake from a small ceramic cup that never seemed to go empty no matter how much she sipped, Mr. Tanaka let Anita know that he wanted her to take it easy for the first three days before she met with lawyers. The reporters and photographers would follow her throughout the days and evenings, but they would not be invasive to her daily activities. Mr. Tanaka had arranged for her to safely exercise and jog through Tokyo. He saw to it that she had a private sightseeing guide for Tokyo, Osaka, and Kyoto (which included visiting temples). Anita learned a lot about Japanese cultures and religions.

On the fourth day, Mr. Tanaka introduced Anita to the Japanese lawyers. Anita had been told by others that she was wasting her time because the lawyers would not hire her as an attorney because she was a woman and too young. As you know, it is not dear Anita's style to listen to gossip or negativity; therefore, she used her confidence and mind to prepare herself to be the best attorney present for the interviews. She did this by practicing her Japanese and learning of their business etiquette. As Mr. Tanaka presented her, one by one, Anita bowed her head and said, "Ohayou gozaimasu" and simultaneously, with both hands, she presented her business card, written in Japanese on one side and English on the other, to each lawyer. She handed them the card Japanese side up. They looked at her card, then Anita and lastly Mr. Tanaka. Once Anita had met all the lawyers, Mr. Tanaka spoke in Japanese, using tones of goodwill, a lengthy introduction of Anita and her accomplishments as an attorney and honorableness as an individual. As he gave the introduction, the lead lawyer, known as the Japanese Lord, remained fixated on Anita and her business card. Incessantly, he would gaze upon Anita, and then slowly lower his eyes to her business card in his hand, remain expressionless, and then slowly raise his eyes back upon Anita. Through the corner of his eyes, he could see the other lawyers' silent connection to Anita's business card. Once Mr. Tanaka completed the introduction, the interview began. Or you might say, the interrogation began, because the Japanese Lord and the other lawyers were very demanding and detail-oriented in their questions (while Anita's business card remained within their sight). Anita had done all her homework, so she was both self-assured and knowledgeable in her answers. Two topics weighed heavily in their questions. One, would you be able to represent us in both the state and federal systems. Anita assured them yes. Two, would you be able to get us punitive damages? Although they may not have wanted to hear her answer, she responded honestly that due to the Geneva Convention, she most likely would not be able to get them punitive damages, but she would definitely put forth her best effort in all attempts to do as such. A wise warrior will always tell another what they need to hear and not what they want to hear. As the line of questions came to a close, the formality of thank yous and bowing of heads began. The Japanese Lord's face reflected reverence in his eyes, trust in his smile, and exhilaration in his bow as he thanked Anita. My dear Anita's words of truth gave her the honor of representing and being of service to the Korean Airlines Flight 007 surviving family members. Mr. Tanaka once more was very proud of his beloved friend, as was I. As a treat for doing a job well done, Mr. Tanaka surprised Anita with an American luncheon of hamburgers, french fries, and orange sodas. Anita laughed happily at the selfless indulgence he had bestowed upon her, but in the back of her mind, she was thinking about how she would love to have Japanese food. As if he was reading her mind, Mr. Tanaka took her and her mother out that evening for a celebration dinner of sushi and sake. So much kindness surrounded dear Anita, as it always has!

My dear Anita stayed in Japan for about a week. She and her mother enjoyed the country and Mr. Tanaka's friendship. He was very generous to Anita with his time, kindness, little gifts, keeping her mother entertained, and introducing her to his insights of the Japanese culture and beliefs. The two of them held a bond that would continue for many years to come. In coming home to the United States, Anita would begin to explore more about the Japanese ways of life and they would begin to play an important role in her future endeavors and lifestyle. I can't wait to tell you of them, but I must wait for now. We dragons get so excited to share our knowledge, but we know, too, that timing must be in the right order to share properly, so please be patient for a little bit longer!

Not too long after she returned to the United States, the Japanese magazine article with the feature of Anita was sent to her by Mr. Tanaka. It was a wonderful article filled with a spellbinding story and bewitching photos. True to her previous words to Mr. Speiser, the article made reference to Speiser Krause law firm many times over. Mr. Speiser smiled and laughed with pure amusement as Anita once more jumped up and down to show him the magazine! He knew she was one in a million and all that she touched turned to gold!

As synchrodestiny would have it, in one of the Japanese magazine photos, dear Anita was shown reading a newspaper that had an article about an airplane whose take-off had been aborted causing injury and death to its passengers and crew. This was the Spantax Flight 995, which would prove to be her next case. The Spantax Flight 995 was leaving the Malaga Airport (approximately five miles from Malaga) for John F. Kennedy International Airport (New York City). As it was picking up speed racing down the runway, vibrations could be felt throughout the plane. The faster the plane raced, the stronger and more severe became the vibrations. After reaching the non-aborting of take-off speed of V1 and seconds per to lifting off the ground, the pilot chose to abort the take-off due to the uncertainty of what was causing the worsening vibration. The fully fueled jet moved at such horrific speed that it was uncontrollable by the flight crew and proceeded to charge beyond the runway onto the field, hitting an airfield aerial installation, then crossed the Malaga-Torremolinos Highway (hitting passing cars), and finally slammed into a railway embankment, which caused the aircraft to ignite into flames. Emergency procedures were implemented, but the limitedness of time and intensifying of flames overpowered the evacuation. Of the 381 passengers and thirteen crew members, there were a total of fifty deaths and 111 injuries (including one ground injury). Investigations revealed that fragments from a recapped tread on a tire at the nose of the plane had become detached, thus causing the extreme vibration.

After several unsuccessful attempts by another Speiser Krause attorney to be given the Spantax Flight 995 cases, Mr. Krause asked Anita to go to Spain and talk with the surviving family members' lawyers. She was ready to go! Shortly after landing in Madrid, Anita met with the Spanish-speaking lawyers and discussed in detail what she and the Speiser Krause law firm could do for their clients. They were intrigued and charmed by Anita's words and granted her the surviving family members' cases. Being Cuban proved to be beautiful once more for Anita because the lawyers wanted an attorney who spoke their language with them and not to them through an interpreter. My dear Anita was still successfully educating others on how smart and wonderful Cubans are no matter what part of the world they may be in. Gracias, mi querida hermosa Anita Aiki Dragon!

While working on both the Korean Airlines Flight 007 and Spantax Flight 995 cases, Anita was spending a lot of time in Texas and Louisiana. She fell in love with Texas with its openness of land and warm, sunny weather. She mentioned this to Mr. Speiser and it was decided, much to Anita's pleasure, that Speiser Krause would open up a branch in Houston, Texas. Dear Anita lost no time in making the move!

Anita did very well with the Korean Airlines Flight 007 and Spantax Flight 995 cases in regard to assuring that the surviving family members were given the necessary compensations needed so they may have a life of well-being and financial security. She did meet one of the surviving family members in person one afternoon. Solemnly, he told her that he was supposed to have been on the Spantax flight, but due to personal conflicts, he had to reschedule. He informed her with pauses of panic in his voice and unforgiving despair in his heart that his mother, father, wife, and two children had given him hugs, waves, smiles, and words of "I love you" as they boarded the flight. Now they were all gone by a horrendous death. His world was empty except for the torment of being a survivor. Anita as a compassionate warrior could feel his pain. It traveled through every cell in her body. It beat mournfully within her heart. Her tears she kept to herself for she knew his sorrow was too great for him to bear his own pain twice. He gave Anita all rights to make all decisions needed regarding his financial compensation. At this moment, money was of no comfort to him. He ended his conversation by saying he was leaving to live on a mountain far away from everything in hopes that the solitude would return peace in his mind and heart. With the handshake of kindness, Anita bid him a fond farewell. Anita's tears fell once he was out of sight. The tears were for him and herself. They helped to cleanse her body and heart and give her understanding to the reasons why she was a compassionate warrior. She knew she must be of service to others in need. She realized, at this time, too, that everything must change (Yin and Yang in motion). This was now a time for change for my dear Anita. Although not completely sure of where she may be of service, Anita knew she must leave Speiser Krause. A wise warrior does not always know where their path may go, but instinctually they know it will lead forward to a grateful land where adventure is always present, learning is in abundance, and love's wonderment creates warmth for all it shines upon.

But before we say good-bye to her time at Speiser Krause, I wanted to share a few funny moments that happened between Anita and Mr. Krause. They had a fantastic business rapport and friendship. When on business trips together, they would meet for breakfast prior to going to court. Mr. Krause was a large man with a hearty appetite. He enjoyed fried eggs, fried potatoes, bacon, sausage, and toast with lots of butter and jelly. Anita, concerned for his health, told him he should not eat that kind of food. That it was very bad for his health. He proceeded to eat his breakfast. The next morning, he ordered the same meal and Anita gave him another dissertation regarding the evils of such a breakfast. On the third morning, the waitress came by and asked Mr. Krause what he would like for breakfast, and through the corner of his eye, he could see Anita preparing to give him another dissertation regarding his choice of breakfast foods. "I am not sure what I want. It would be best that you asked Ms. Arango what I should eat," he replied. Anita ordered him oatmeal and bran muffins! Then there was the time when Anita and Mr. Krause were getting off the plane in New Orleans, and it dawned on him that he was always carrying Anita's luggage. So he stated to her, "Ms. Arango, I am a senior partner of the law firm. Do you really think it is appropriate that I should be carrying your luggage?" Anita just smiled a dragon's friendly smile of gratitude and what will be will be. Mr. Krause understood and kindly gave her one nod from his head and continued walking forward with her luggage. Things balance, though! Like the time Mr. Krause was running behind to catch his flight. Anita was already at the airport when he called her stating he was running late and to have the plane held for him. My dear Anita knew not to ask Mr. Krause questions, but to simply do as he said; therefore, she replied, "Yes, sir." As time passed there was still no Mr. Krause and she was in the boarding line moving forward. Time was running out and she knew they were not going to hold the plane for anyone. Quickly, she dropped her handbag, allowing all its contents to fall all over the boarding gate's floor. Slowly, she picked the items up and even dropped a few more back to the floor. Anything to stall for time. Suddenly, running out of breath, Mr. Krause came around the corner to get in line. Once on the plane, dear Anita relaxed with a glass of red wine as Mr. Krause took a quick power nap!

In leaving Speiser Krause Anita did not leave law, at least not at first. She started her own radio talk show called Preguntar Al Abogado (Ask the Lawyer). It was a successful talk show where those in need would call in and ask for law advice. Many of these individuals would come to Anita in person and discuss further their concerns and needs regarding workplace injuries. Most of the clients were undocumented workers who believed they had no workplace rights. Anita helped to educate them (the way of a warrior) that they did have rights and she assisted them in obtaining compensation for their "on the job" injuries. She continued to assist in this manner for quite some time. The Yin and Yang spirit inside her, though, was gently and constantly reminding her that change was to be in her future. The word "equanimity" kept coming into Anita's mind. Mr. Tanaka's world of Japanese cultures and beliefs flowed into her consciousness. Her love for Confucius filled her heart. Being a soul with an adventurous nature, Anita focused on a new not yet named path that required she has a warrior's mental calmness, a dragon's composure, and a shaman's evenness of temper (in all situations). The universe had just given my dear Anita a scholarship to a university way up high!

Chapter 10

Advancing Anita

Philosophy in Motion

Just as little bluebirds fly across the sky, my dear Anita's heart was rising toward new adventures found from her past's steadfast inquisitiveness. Her dearly loved father had inspired in her beliefs of truth, justice, and principles for herself and toward others. As a little girl, these high-level standards were reinforced from her father's nightly readings of Pinocchio. Remember? Then entered her father's own powerful words strongly emphasizing that the best path was always the one of the natural way (which embraced honesty, integrity, healthy eating, no medications, a natural look that included no facial makeup, and a good posture) and that happiness was a state of mind. Anita was always surrounded by love and happiness, which gave her an abundance of energy and freedom to be inquisitive on her quest of learning more and more of her life's path. From her father, too, came the words of Confucius. Confucius, a Chinese philosopher during the Zhou Dynasty, gave prominence to justice, genuineness, and personal morality. As a philosopher, he was a teacher who believed that education was a process of continuous self-improvement of one's knowledge. Dear Anita and Confucius were spiritually connected. To be able to serve others successfully and beneficially, one must educate themselves of all that is needed to learn of the world (which is forever changing) and of their own self (which is forever growing). One must be able to work successfully within to be able to work beneficially for those without. The principles of Confucius led my dear Anita to the Chinese teachings of Lao-tzu (Tao Te Ching) and I-Ching (also known as Book of Changes). Beautiful, beautiful teachings of self, simplicities of truth and guidance for moral decision-making.

I need to tell you of a tale about dear Anita on the day that she purchased her yellow I-Ching book. When consulting the I-Ching one may either use fifty yarrow stalks or three coins. My dear Anita opted for the three coins, for they would be more readily available at times of readings than yarrow stalks (her yang side of logic). Also, Anita has always been a believer in the number nine. Three is a derivative of nine being divided by three (her yin side of congruity). My dear Anita has always had an even flow of balance! With the I-Ching in her hand, she walked Jones Beach, allowing the sand and water to playfully fall upon and wash away from her toes and feet as she searched for the coins and contemplated the secrets to be unfolded to her from the book. While walking she met a man who was alone and enveloped in his thoughts. He mentioned to her that he was perplexed due to an incident that had recently taken place. As an oncologist and medical director, he had diagnosed a patient with terminal cancer. Upon having received the news, the patient left his office and jumped from the 50th story of the building. Suddenly, as if destined by fate, a strong gust of wind broke her fall and she landed on a lower floor balcony (with minor injuries to her legs). Shortly thereafter, in running further tests, in preparation for treatment, the doctor found that the cancer was gone. What had taken her cancer away? The strong gust of wind? The power of surviving death and a new will to live? Had the cells in her body been changed by the impact of the fall? These were the questions the man was asking himself. For my dear Anita, it opened the pathway to her fascination with sages and scientists. My dear Anita's movements of mind have always been spinning forward in thought!

After having said goodbye to the man, she continued to walk the beach as waves of water rolled over her feet and waves of thought rolled over her mind. Somehow, someway there must be a connection between scientific medicines if you will, and those which are more of a holistic nature. Many years later Anita's thoughts would return, expecting an answer. The answers would be found in her post practicing law learnings. Anita's mind suddenly stopped thinking of medicines as her eyes viewed a silvery spot in the sand. As she approached, Anita discovered three coins. Three little dimes (which she still uses). With little anxiety and lots of excitement, Anita proceeded to open her I-Ching and toss her three coins six times (which makes for eighteen!) to learn the art of divination.

My dear Anita soon learned of the tarot deck, which originated in Europe, and periodically would look to it for guidance for herself and others. Eventually, Anita stopped reading for others because sometimes the messages were not of a positive certainty and she did not favor being the messenger of bad news. One day, Anita's father surprised her with a tarot deck that had been designed by Salvador Dali. The cards are beautiful with Dali's surrealistic artwork (created especially for the tarots), and the backs are covered in his signature and edged in gold. Dear Anita keeps them in a clear glass case surrounded in gold metal trim. She also keeps them near and dear to her heart beside her father's love.

Anita discovered, too, the animal medicine cards (from the teaching of the Native Americans and Mayan traditions). This is the art of divination practiced to assist one in finding their personal path of self-empowerment, understanding, and strength, through the medicine powers found in the animal kingdom. One learns to heal from that which is blocking them and to connect with the universe through the traits and habits of Mother Earth's animal children.

My dear Anita became an enthusiast of yoga. Many believe that yoga is just a form of toning and burning calories, which is true, but there is so much more to be found through this discipline. Yoga, originally from ancient India, is combining the physical, mental, and spiritual aspects of oneself through the practice of daily stretches, body poses, deep breathing, and meditation, thus strengthening your body, mind, and soul.

Anita, from her days of Catholic school, was well versed in the teachings of Jesus and the torment he endured so others may be relieved of their sufferings and find peace in heaven's afterlife of immortality. Her favorite saint was and continues to be Saint Anthony. Not so much because he is the patron saint of lost things, but due to the fact that there are so many men named Antonio in her family! "Who else could it be?" she will kiddingly say to you! My dear Anita's humor causes me to smile and chuckle again! Also, my dear Anita has always been adorned by love and to her, Saint Anthony is a patron saint of lost love finding lost love. How beautiful!

Through her knowledge of Confucius and the Tao, Anita was introduced to the world of Buddha and the Asian philosophy of Buddhism. She learned of the Four Noble Truths and Eightfold Path.

Do you see how dear Anita has the intuitive manners of allowing all beliefs to come to her? She has never been rude or disrespectful to any beliefs of religion or enlightenment. No slamming of doors or harsh goodbyes. She has compassionately maintained a continuity of esteem and admiration for all. Love lives in every word, thought, and movement that has flowed to and from her regarding the knowledge of all theologies or philosophies of enlightenment. Dear Anita has the blessings of gratitude all around her.

Gratitude attracts gratitude. One of Anita's blessings of gratitude was Mr. Tanaka. Their friendship was one of respect, trust, kindness, and giving from the heart. Mr. Tanaka gave Anita a heart-filled introduction to the Japanese teachings of Zen where she learned of the Nine Principles. She practiced Zen meditation styles and esoteric methods. Zen helped to reiterate to Anita the importance of being calmly and consistently aware of and in the flow of the moment. Dear Anita, always the ready student, read books on Zen. Through her readings, she was reacquainted with a subject matter of great interest from her past—Aikido. She began to read the book *Aikido and the Harmony of Nature*. She took notes and highlighted portions of the text as she read. She reread the book and took more notes and re-highlighted the same lines, again, and other lines, as well (highlighting them in a new color, of course!). Which is very symbolic in the respect that she was seeing the same words in a more powerful way or with an additional meaning to her. The change of colors indicates a new awareness of growth. And isn't that what we all truly want? To be aware and to grow! The compassionate warrior in my dear Anita had just signed up to attend graduate school at the University of the Universe, and her path was to unfold great mysteries of herself and those beings who master the movements of love and kindness.

Mysteries, though, must be learned patiently and lovingly over time. So for now, like Anita at the time, you must wait to learn of Anita's Aikido Universe. I will give you a hint, though! Aikido is one of the most beautiful words you will ever learn. For within the word AIKIDO, you will discover the meaning of: AI—harmony, KI—spirit, DO—the way. Thought-provoking, intriguing, and enlightening all at the same time, isn't it?!

Chapter 11

Chinese Medicine Anita

Always Have Respect and Trust for the Body

My dear Anita has always been at one with her body. She is very attentive and astute when it comes to the communication she has with her body. In her daily prayers and meditations, dear Anita gives loving thanks to all that is near and dear to her. Of course, everything is near and dear to Anita. It does not matter where in the universe it may be, for it is always only a breath and thought away. She gives love and thanks to her father, mother, and Abuela Ana. She gives love and thanks to all the many friends who have enriched her life. She gives love and thanks to the earth, water, trees, flowers, and animals. Harmoniously, Anita gives love and thanks for her life's journey and all that is in the universe. Anita also gives love and thanks to her body, mind, and soul. She is most grateful for having a body of excellent health, a nonjudgmental mind that is forever eager and open to learning and sharing all that leads to her path, and a compassionate, soul-filled love and kindness. Also, within my dear Anita's body, mind, and soul, she has Chi (Chinese for the flow of life's energy) and this is what helped to bring Chinese medicine onto Anita's path.

Although it is true that Anita has always been of excellent health, there was a time when her body indicated to her that it was a little out of positioning and in need of a minor balance and aligning. She had been informed about the technique of Rolfing. Rolfing is a holistic approach (done in ten sessions) that is a form of deep tissue massage at the soft tissue level that works with the connective tissue and fascia. Unlike chiropractic, it deals with the whole body and not just a specified part. Anita began her sessions and almost immediately began to feel a difference. This was fascinating to her in the respect that the technique of Rolfing was dealing with her body as a whole and not compartmentalizing it. She was a participant in her Rolfing sessions. As her Rolfer rolled and lifted her tissues, she would concentrate on certain body movements and breathing techniques. The joint effort of fine-tuning of her body was allowing any possible blockages within her tissues to be released and create more powerful and healthier energy. My dear Anita had questions and more questions as the Rolfing sessions continued to proceed. Soon, her questions would bring her to being introduced to Dr. Song.

Dr. Song was a Chinese medicine doctor from China with many years of experience. He was a graduate from Sichuan Provincial Research Traditional Medical Institute and Chengdu College of Traditional Chinese Medical Science. Dr. Song took an instant appreciation to Anita and her many questions regarding energy. Dr. Song pleasantly smiled as he answered her questions and tied them into the fundamentals of Chinese medicine. Dear Anita's Rolfing questions were soon turning into Chinese medicine questions! Dr. Song became enthralled by Anita's intriguing questions. He began to realize as soon as he answered one question that the answer itself would be an opening to another question. In answering her questions he gave her a quick, basic explanation of Chinese medicine. He explained to Anita that Chinese medicine (or as some refer to it, Eastern medicine) had originated in ancient China and that it dealt with the individual as a whole to include body, mind, and soul. Chinese medicine attempted, through a more holistic and preventative approach of healthy diet, herbs, exercise, acupuncture, and massages (such as Rolfing), to prevent disease before it came to be. Dr. Song explained that Western medicine dealt more with the specific disease at the time of the ailment, and treatment was primarily through drugs or vaccines.

Now, dear Anita, with kindness listened to Dr. Song's words so she may learn more, even though she was essentially aware of the Eastern and Western differences. Her father had taught her well regarding the path of the natural way, which included a healthy diet and no medications. He ate wholesome, nutritious foods and did not take medicines. To him, the best medicine came in the form of sleep (whether it be a power nap or a full night's slumber). Her Abuela Ana, having been a curandera, had guided Anita in the necessities of taking preventative measures regarding ailments by impressing upon her the importance of healing herbs. Dear Anita has always had an internal atmosphere filled with love, kindness, and happiness, which keeps her body in excellent health.

There is an old Chinese story regarding one's internal atmosphere and how it can save and protect. Long ago, two sisters unknowingly were given tainted rice. The sister who was mean in thought and disrespect of all near her fell gravely ill that evening following dinner. Her body was already filled with toxins of unkind thoughts and negative attitudes that were swiftly drawn to the contamination within the rice, thus causing her mind, body, and spirit to be overpowered by too much disease. She passed before the morning's sun had risen. The sister who was filled with love and happiness slept soundly throughout the night and awoke renewed to the sun rising and the birds singing. The poison within the rice she ate was compassionately surrounded by little powerful warriors of love and happiness, which caused the toxins to quickly dissipate and never enter the cells of her body or heart. In Chinese medicine, one's internal atmosphere is a very important role in one's health. Happiness makes for healthiness!

Anita's Chi was aligning with Chinese medicine. It was as if Confucius had whispered his words of wisdom into her ears. For she remembered in his writings (and of the Tao) that one should put things in order to prevent trouble before it appears. And was not Confucius a full-time teacher and student? In her centeredness with the Tao, Anita knew the time was now to become a full-time student in Chinese medicine. She asked Dr. Song to be her teacher. Without pause or thought he firmly replied, "Classes shall begin first thing tomorrow morning." The reading of textbooks, lectures, and taking of notes were to begin once more for Anita. Enthusiasm and excitement filled my dear Anita's body, mind, and soul!

Dr. Song's lesson plans for Anita were very well organized. He began first with the theory of Yin and Yang and how it is the foundation for Chinese medicine as it relates to diagnosis and treatment. Yin and Yang consists of the dualism found in everything that exists in the universe; thus it has to do with all, including Chinese medicine. Yin and Yang's opposing and complementary forces are what create the energies within our bodies. They create our Chi. Chi energy is found in everything that makes our bodies. Our organs have Chi. The space in between our organs have Chi. Our bones, tissues, and muscles have Chi. Our personality and emotions have Chi. Yin must have Yang, and vice versa, to exist. As a rule, Yin and Yang remain harmonious with one another, yet like the seasons they are forever changing. And with these changes, they may become temporarily imbalanced. This is when disease may begin to set in. The premise of Chinese medicine is to be in awareness of the body's Yin and Yang balances so that preventative medicine may come into action prior to any symptoms that may lead to disease. It also means having an internal atmosphere of happiness and love within the body. This type of good energy allows one to keep a healthy mental status of believing that the treatment of Chinese medicine will keep you healthy.

In Chinese medicine there are no or yes answers to questions. There is no absolute. There is no right or wrong. There is Chi, though. Chi is of the utmost importance. Rather than get into the specifics, as one might do with Western medicine, let me tell you of a story of an elderly man who smoked. He smoked every afternoon. He would go outside and sit under a large willow tree in his chair that faced a brook where fish swam, turtles basked in the sun, and ducks paddled atop the water. As he smoked his mind would go away from his daily stresses and concerns. As he inhaled, he would feel the sun and light breeze against his skin. His eyes would gaze upon the carefreeness of the turtles and ducks. His ears would hear the soft splashing of the brook's water passing by. His mind would go to happy thoughts of his wife, children, grandchildren, and great-grandchildren. He became one with all that was around him. Beauty surrounding beauty. One day, after a visit to his Western physician, he was informed that he must stop smoking due to the possibility that damage may have or may begin to take place in his lungs and body. In short, he was banned from cigarettes. Without his cigarettes, he had no need or desire to go outside. He no longer had his "at one" with nature's beauty and his happy thoughts. He remained indoors trapped with his daily stress and concerns. His good Chi became stagnate allowing for depression set in. Sadly, within six months he passed. Cigarettes did not kill him. Depression did. For this elderly man, cigarettes gave him moments of freedom and tranquility. You must understand that as he smoked, his internal atmosphere was that of happiness and love. He was surrounded by an outside world of beauty and peace. This practice kept him free of harm and his body in harmony. Yin and Yang in motion. He smoked outdoors in a world of peace to counteract a smokeless indoor world of stress.

Please, let me explain the basics of how Yin and Yang work hand-in-hand with Chinese medicine. As you are aware the seasons change every year. We go from spring to summer to autumn to winter and then begin the cycle over again with spring. We must have change to have life. With change, we must have balance. We have change every day of our lives whether we see it or not. My dear Anita brought an example of change to my attention that I found to be most thought-provoking. She laid a pair of reading glasses (not hers, for she has perfect vision) down on her desk and asked me if they were changing. I responded no. She then asked me, if she was to leave them on her desk for a thousand years, would they change. I responded yes. She then asked me, when did they begin to change? Anita, always being quick, and before I could answer, responded, "They are changing now (you just can't see the change yet)." She spoke the truth! Change is constant!

Thus Yin and Yang are forever changing. Within the Yin and Yang theory are the Five Elements, which consist of wood, fire, earth, metal, and water. These five elements are considered to be the essential elements to everything in the universe, to include the human body's organs and their interaction with one another. For example, the earth creates metals (such as gold and silver) and it also absorbs water, which in turn creates wood. Thus, the earth has the Yin and Yang quality of flowing its energy into something to be (gold and silver) or from something that already is (water). Think of it this way. A beautiful multi-jewel-colored hummingbird (the earth) with its fast-moving wings (Chi energy) has inside itself two tiny eggs (gold and silver) as it hovers, like a miniature helicopter, over a pink flower while drinking the nectar (water) from the blossom. On its beak, it has pollinated nectar (water), which, as the hummingbird flies to another blossom, drips to the ground, giving nourishment for future healthy flowers. The power of good Chi continuously moves forward.

Another facet of Chinese medicine is the ancient philosophy of Feng Shui. As Chinese medicine is the interaction and balance of Yin and Yang with good Chi throughout the organs and body, Feng Shui is the interaction and balance of Yin and Yang with good Chi throughout one's self and surroundings (home and office). The practice of Feng Shui (which includes the five elements of wood, fire, earth, metal, and water) is accomplished by the proper directional placement of furniture, objects, and colors within the home (or office) to allow Chi energy to freely flow. In turn the Chi energy within your surroundings will flow through you and in all that you think and do on a daily basis. The good Chi energy will create a prosperous world for you in friendships, love, health, money, and personal growth. There was a man who was filled with love and happiness in his heart, but his outer world was of dismay due to the doubts that he knowingly and unknowingly created. He longed to have a calm world of personal success to include friendships, love, and prosperity. My dear Anita introduced him to the artistry of Feng Shui, and his world began to change into peaceful beauty. He organized his home to be free of unnecessary clutter to allow for natural flows of energy. He cleaned all the windows in his home to allow more natural light and positive energies to come inside. He removed the television and all work-related objects from his bedroom, which allowed for a good night's rest. He kept the bathroom doors closed to keep wealth from being flushed away. In the southwest corner of his home, he placed small gifts friends had given him and objects of love to allow the flow of friends and love to constantly surround his life. In the southeast corner of his home, he placed earth and water objects (a small bamboo plant and trickling water fountain) to allow the flow of wealth to enter and become well planted within his home. In the center of his home, he placed fresh flowers of blues and purples to allow for good health to be abundantly present. Dear Anita gave him a small Kannon statue so his home would remain compassionately and lovingly protected and embraced with happiness. Soon his world was filled with the love and laughter of good friends, loved ones, prosperous business negotiations, sleep's restfulness, serenity, and the removal of doubts and negative thoughts that had previously held him back from the full beauties that had always been within his realm. My dear Anita in the selfless manner of Kannon had used her mind of knowledge (like that of Kannon's bottle of wisdom) and heart of tenderness and love (like that of Kannon's weeping willow twig) to spread the creative forces of joy and happiness into that man's world. My dear, dear Anita, how I love you for your never-ending and generous energies of love, compassion, and full-hearted concern for others' well-being. You have the remarkable gift of changing one's silent sufferings to thunderous laughter of jubilation and life's riches!

Another important aspect of Chinese medicine is the communication between the physician and the patient. Unlike Western medicine, the Chinese medicine physician encourages patient conversation and will ask many questions. It is by hearing the patient's words and the sound of their voice that the physician can be better in sync and involved in treating preventative care. Dear Anita was telling me of two incidents, once with her father and once with her, where the Western physician either did not ask questions or chose not to listen. Anita's father, Mr. Arango, was a man who was sensitive to others needing others. There was a certain commercial that entailed reaching out to loved ones that would make him a little teary-eyed. Yet, he was very macho in the sense that he believed men did not belong in the kitchen when it came to cooking or cleaning, but he was usually the first one at the dinner table and ready for telling and sharing great jokes! Mr. Arango had a well-rounded internal atmosphere of compassion, judgment, wisdom, and happiness. For a brief time, he was having stomach ailments for which he went to the doctor. The doctor asked him very few questions and proceeded to write him a prescription. He came home and told dear Anita about his visit and the doctor's solution being a prescription, and should that not work, an invasive procedure would be performed. Now, you know how Anita is with her love of questions. She proceeded to ask her father many questions regarding not just the doctor visit, but what all he was doing on a day-to-day basis and if anything had changed. She also asked him about his diet. Was he eating anything different? He stated no, at first. And then he realized he had begun, a few weeks earlier, to get up in the middle of the night to drink tomato juice with lots of olives. Dear Anita explained to him that even though the tomato juice and olives were healthy, as a whole, he was consuming too much acidity at one time, thus the reason for his stomach problem. She recommended that he discontinue having his midnight snack of juice and olives. He stopped and within a couple of days, his body was back to normal. No prescription drugs needed.

The second incident involved dear Anita's health due to work-related stress. She was in the midst of a seven-week trial where the opposing team was proving to be vindictive and mean to those who were not in agreement with their points of view. My dear Anita, always being one of truth, continued to stand firm to the ground regarding her forthright and honest stance in the case. She had a rash break out on the side of her face (near her eye). She went to several Western doctors for answers. Anita realized that none of them asked her questions, so she took it on herself to explain all that was going on with her and the possible causes for her rash. She realized that not only did the doctors not ask her questions, but they were not listening to her words. As she talked, they had a pen and pad in hand, but not to document her concerns. The pen and pad were to write a prescription. The diagnoses ranged from not too serious to "you may not have long to live." Anita, with her sense of humor, told the doctor that she had too much on her plate to do and that she did not have time to die and there must be another solution. He wrote her a prescription, which she hesitantly took. Within minutes her face was swelling up. She called the doctor and he only told her to stop taking the medicine. Anita was not going to let the rash or drugs kill her! Besides, with her internal atmosphere of love and happiness, there was no way death was going to take place. She was able to finally get hold of Dr. Song (he had been out of the country) and explain to him what was going on. He asked her question after question regarding her rash. He listened intensely as she relayed to him all her information. He had questions of his own, which she answered. It was decided that he would give her a single session of acupuncture treatment. Within a couple of days, the rash was gone. Dr. Song had released all toxins through her skin. Anita did state that shortly after the acupuncture, she began to feel heat and a fever. This was a good thing, though, because the heat of the fever was working with her body in removing the toxins of stress (which had caused the stagnation of her good Chi). Anita also mentioned that on the following day, in running her errands, her energy was not at its highest, which caused her to feel slightly drained. Anita did not take this as a negative, though; on the contrary, she took it as another good thing because it opened her to creative thoughts regarding ailments. Anita had always been the epitome of excellent health and by temporarily having an ailment she was able to connect with how others must feel when they are ill. She understood how being drained of physical energy could play havoc on one's life and activities. She, too, remembered Albert Einstein's definition of insanity, which meant doing the same thing over and over again and expecting different results. She had just experienced his definition of insanity by going to several Western doctors where none asked questions or listened and all chose to treat her with prescriptions. She knew that true health and wellness was to be found through her continued studies of Chinese medicine.

Now, as I mentioned before, it is very important for us to keep an internal atmosphere within us. Sometimes, though, our surroundings, whether we realize it or not, can disrupt our internal atmosphere. Anita knew of a person who was always nervous at work. It was as if they were walking on slippery floors and about to fall. This person would literally jump up high and out of their chair, in fright, whenever someone walked into their office. It did not matter if the entering individual was a coworker, stranger, or friend, for he would still shake and jump. The way Anita explained him to me, he reminded of the cartoon character of the nervous cat who would jump straight from the floor to the ceiling and cling by their nails as they uncontrollably shook in fear. Dear Anita being the number one detective in solving problems went one day to his office. Being polite and conscientious regarding his fear, she called him about two minutes before entering his office, so there would be no surprises. When she arrived, the door was open and she could see his back as he sat behind his desk focused on his computer screen. Dear Anita softly said, "Hello, Daniel." He did not flinch and kept on working. Anita walked closer to his desk and once more softly said, "Hello, Daniel." No reaction. Wanting to ensure that she did not frighten him, Anita took a pencil from a small table near his desk and dropped it to the floor next to him. He slightly turned back and looked down at the pencil and saw Anita's fuchsia shoes, and smiled for he knew Anita had arrived. He apologized for having not realized sooner that she was in the room. "Daniel, it is no wonder that you are nervous all the time. You have your back to the door and your front to the wall," proclaimed Anita. "You need to turn your desk around so you can see and hear what's going on around you." So with that, they turned the desk around to face the door. She adjusted his computer screen so he could still see in front of him. Placed the printer near his desk. Moved the phone nearer to his reach (and softened the volume). Got him a stronger bulb for his desk lamp so he could read better. They organized all the papers on and in his desk so he would be better able to instantly find what he needed. Lastly, Anita opened the blinds to the window, allowing natural sunlight to come into the office. By the end of the day, Daniel was a man whose fear and nervousness had been replaced with laughter and happiness. Anita knew the art of Feng Shui, and with a few changes in location and placement of Daniel's office belongings, good Chi immediately began to flow throughout Daniel (and his office). Nervousness problem solved and gone forever!

The turning of Daniel's desk also conveys the importance of one properly communicating with oneself and all that is about (as Chinese medicine reveals). At first glance, we can see the human forms of communication with the desk facing the door, the phone, and the computer. There is also the communication with nature and the universe. Physically, Anita had opened the window blinds to let the sunlight into the office. Spiritually, she had opened the window blinds for Daniel to hear nature's voice and to see the universe's soul. (My dear Anita has opened the universe's soul for so many!) The illuminating sun shared with Daniel the words of beauty and good health (all that natural vitamin D). He could feel the sun upon him, which allowed him to be a part of the outdoors. He could see and hear the different birds singing with one another. When it rained he could hear the sound of the water falling on the plants, trees, and ground. He could hear how nature talks, nourishes, and protects all the little beings that are the universe. He began to take note of all that was happening outside his window and realized how fascinating and inspiring nature's wisdom was to him. He soon understood that he was the universe too. He began to communicate, as dear Anita does with hers, with his own body. He began to pay attention to his emotions and feelings of health. He learned that he must listen to his body to have good health. Not only listen but trust it as well. He remembered that Anita had once told him about three men—Mr. Wise, Mr. Intellectual, and Mr. Foolish. Mr. Wise was the man who would hear the truth and move forward with the information. Mr. Intellectual was the man who would hear the truth and analyze it. Mr. Foolish was the man who heard the truth and only laughed and scoffed at it. Daniel chose to become Mr. Wise. Chinese medicine teaches that we all need to become Mr. or Ms. Wise to live a life of excellent health. My dear Anita, thank you for sharing your love and wisdom with all those who come into your world. My brain and heart are equally overfilling with happiness because of you and your love.

So what do you think of Chinese medicine? Is it not thought-provoking and energizing? My dear Anita found it to be delightfully enthralling! She studied with Dr. Song for eleven years. He would come to her home twice a week with a lecture prepared and textbook in hand to educate Anita in all there was to know about Chinese medicine. Anita as the avid student, in the same manner as the element of earth absorbs water, thirsted for all there was to learn. In her learning, she used the element of water and grew wood...lots and lots of trees of Chinese knowledge are within her (and continue to grow). My dear Anita graduated from the Chengdu University of Traditional Chinese Medicine with two degrees: Chinese Medicine Treatment and Chinese Medicine Diagnosis. Anita was the first foreign student to graduate from Chengdu University (located in Sichuan, China). She also received from Clayton College of Natural Health the degree of Doctor of Naturopathy (with high honors!) after six years of extensive learning. My dear Anita successfully became a Chinese medicine doctor. How very, very proud of her I am.

Anita's knowledge of Chinese medicine did not stop there. Dr. Song shared and entrusted her with the knowledge of the secret ancient Chinese healing art of Chu Jing. In these ancient healings live the secret teachings of how one can always keep oneself in excellent health. It encompasses the elements of metal and water. Metal being the Chu Jing tools and water being our bodies (for the good Chi energy to flow). The Chu Jing tools are beautiful healing tools. Anita had them handmade in China. She also asked her father to enrich them with his regal touch of craftsmanship to allow for the best in benefiting health. Mr. Arango, having been an illustrious jeweler, was able to get them to be of impeccable quality. FYI…Mr. Arango was a well-respected man within the New York Jewelry District. He was a goy (from Cuba) and given the chivalrous nickname of "the Jew of the Caribbean!" His trustworthiness gave him the prestigious responsibility of being the one person given the combination to a main jewelry vault in the New York Jewelry District. He worked many years with a prestigious, well-known jewelry company, creating one-of-a-kind pieces of gold and platinum jewelry encrusted with diamonds, sapphires, rubies, and emeralds. Many years ago, he made Anita a beautiful, large, gold dragon broach covered in diamonds with rubies for the eyes. Mr. Arango created a breathtaking dragon masterpiece! Also, let's not forget he brought to life another breathtaking dragon masterpiece—dear Anita! Mr. Arango had a dragon within him, too, as you can see through all his outstanding qualities! Wait, though, I am getting ahead of myself now in regard to the World of Dragons, which we will be discussing soon.

Anita and Dr. Song's honorable intentions for the secret ancient Chinese healing art of Chu Jing were to educate others so they may become true healing artist within themselves, so they, too, may have forever excellent health. My dear Anita is a compassionate samurai warrior, who through kindness, awareness, and love for all has created an encircling world of service to others so they may have the betterment of all that is empowering, including the good Chi's healing energy of excellent health. Mucho amor y excelente salud para ti siempre mi querida Anita!

My dear Anita and I learned long ago that Chinese medicine is like placing wind chimes in the center bagua of one's spirit where it will be harmoniously blown by the flow of life's good energy throughout the body as it resonates outward with powerful tones of health, goodwill, and kindness for all to hear and enjoy the peaceful vibrations of the universe's love.

In discussing Chinese medicine with you, it reminds me of a beautiful and loving song that Anita and I sing with each other. It has four simple yet powerful lines:

Happiness runs in a circular motion
Life is like a little boat upon a sea
Everything is a part of everything anyway
You can have it all if you let yourself be.

We love to sing this song over and over. It brings such happiness and joy to us. And this happiness and joy, like the melodic percussions of wind chimes, gracefully swirls through our bodies letting us know that we are as one with the universe and all the beauty it holds. So much beauty for all!

Dear Anita and her Abuela Ana inside the quincalla.

Dear Anita with her Mami and Papi.

Papi and his Dear Anita.

Welcome to my dojo!

A dragon has her wings!

Chapter 12

Reflections / Anita

Sukoshi Tsu Tsu (Little by Little)

My dear Anita, whose mind, body, and soul are always spinning forward in the world of awareness, decided it was time to reflect on her inner strengths and spirituality. Chinese medicine had opened to her a fascinating new world of knowledge regarding the Eastern and Western beliefs of not only self but of the correlation between science and spirituality. As always, she had many questions. Unlike other questions she had before, these questions were coming from deep within who she had become through her life's learnings and adventures. She was not questioning herself. Far from that. Her questions were those of one's consciousness. Where in the body does one's consciousness live? What forms does one's consciousness take regarding one's thoughts, actions, and volitions? How is one's consciousness connected with the universe? Where would this consciousness be taking her?

My dear Anita had heard the name Dr. Deepak Chopra and set out to explore his world of alternative medicine and spirituality. Anita met with him for answers to her questions of consciousness. She attended many of his seminars and courses. One of the courses she took was that of Laughing. Oh my goodness, she really enjoyed that course. All she did was laugh (for hours). She got to be a grown-up little girl. She went running around (or should I say flying around) the huge classroom pretending she was a laughing airplane! Anita's laughter was her plane's fuel (energy)! She would begin with her arms (being her wings) low to the ground, ready for the take-off; then she would lift up and zoom forward, bringing her body and arms (wings) up high (into a playful sky) and fly all around the room, landing in front of people and making them laugh with her laughter and make-believe aviation antics. She even did a few spiral loops for more fun and laughter. For a brief moment, it reminded her of Mr. D'Angelone (her flying instructor) and her past freedoms in the big sky, and she began to smile and release even more laughter. Fun, fun, fun is what Anita was experiencing! Laughter is a great way to get people to relax and become filled with happiness. Especially when it comes full-heartedly from the soul as Anita's laughter comes! Later that day, she even did laughter meditation. What a high-spirited way for Anita to connect with the universe and her higher self.

Later, during the seminar, Anita joined in with the Seven Spiritual Laws of Yoga course. How invigorating for her soul, mind, and body! She and her classmates would get up early in the morning, as the sun was rising, and begin with sun salutations (using the energy of the sun in unison with the movement of her body in various poses, breaths, and sutras). With the yoga movements of her body, my dear Anita was and is able to bring forth the seven spiritual laws of yoga into a consciousness that remains with her throughout the day, allowing her to always be at her best and succeed in all that she pursues. Anita would be dressed so nicely in colorful yoga outfits. Her favorite was her black leotard with a gold and black leopard-style yoga jacket and matching headscarf. This is no wonder because leopards represent great speed and strength, power, confidence, perseverance, and a successful warrior. She also wore around her waist a beautiful solid gold chain that would glisten with her spirit's energy when shined upon by the early morning's sun. Her father made the gold chain for Anita when she was an honor student in high school. The intertwining gold links give my dear Anita perfect style and protection. She has worn this gold chain with continuity from the very first day her father gave it to her.

My dear Anita also became involved with the healing practice of Primordial Sound Meditation, which allows for restful awareness (through the stillness of the physical body and opening of awareness through a silent mind). In her silent mind and unique mantra, dear Anita was able to connect to the universal consciousness of opening up her energies to more creativity, love, intuition, and infinite possibilities. She became certified as a Primordial Sound Meditation counselor and assisted others in connecting with their higher selves and universal consciousness.

As dear Anita continued with her Chopra teachings, she was learning more and more about consciousness. She attended the Sages and Scientists symposium, where the scientists and spiritualists of the world sat together and discussed the oneness of the universe and how it ties in with quantum physics and spirituality. She was understanding that consciousness lives within every cell of the body (much like mitochondria are the powerhouse of the cell). And that consciousness, whether knowingly or unknowingly, is involved with all of one's thoughts, which ultimately turn into actions that create to our future. Having true consciousness of all that is surrounding ourselves is the link to the universe. It is the link to Cosmic Consciousness.

Cosmic Consciousness is the link between Science and Spirituality. The Chopra seminar had a compelling and thought-provoking symposium called Sages and Scientists that Anita eagerly and with self-insight attended. Top spiritualists and neuroscientists came together, before the audience, to discuss the intertwining of spiritual beliefs and modern-day sciences. They correlated the qualities of quantum physics and the connection of oneness for everything that exists within the universe. The spiritualists and neuroscientists explained that through our thoughts and perceptions lies our future and interconnection with others and objects within the universe. An angelic explanation of this may be told through the eyes of my dear Anita's love for her Abuela Ana. As you know, dear Anita and her Abuela Ana have a bond of love between them that will never come to an end. When they would talk, each would naturally know how to finish the sentence for the other. They connected as though they were one. Remember how Anita on her way home from the law firm used to stop at her Abuela Ana's home and she would bless and protect Anita from any harm or danger? Anita did the same for her. As time moved forward, Abuela Ana moved into Anita's home so Anita could bless her with a safe, carefree, and loving life for the remainder of her years. You see, Abuela Ana was becoming very old in human years (fortunately, though, in spirit years she was still a very young wondrous woman). Dear Anita gave Abuela Ana the top floor of her home so she may live on the top of the world with a magical view. Abuela Ana's room was graciously decorated with all her earthly possessions in celebration of her life's journey. Abuela Ana had a rare, precious gift of an enlarged heart filled with love and happiness that flowed good energy within her body and granted her another precious gift of being able to see all that could be seen whether of the physical or spiritual world. Yes, Abuela Ana was living on the top of the world! Anita knew that the earthly time between her and Abuela Ana was nearing a close. Anita successfully did all she could to keep her Abuela Ana healthy and happy for many years.

One evening, Anita went to the music hall to listen to music. She had a wonderful evening and enjoyed the music immensely. In putting on her wrap to leave, she noticed that the large center diamond of her ring had fallen out of its setting. She began to look for the diamond and then suddenly thought of her Abuela Ana. Anita said quietly to herself that the diamond may remain with the universe in exchange for more time with Abuela Ana. With the radiance of love Anita began to leave the music hall. Suddenly, someone tapped her on the shoulder and said, "This belongs to you." He handed her the diamond. Anita knew her beloved Abuela Ana would be leaving soon.

The following morning, Abuela Ana told Anita that it was time to say goodbye. Abuela Ana longed to be with her husband, Pedro, and other family members who had passed on. She told Anita that she would always be with her. "Look into the sky at night, my dear, and you will see a bright yellow star. This will be me. I will be there for you," she whispered lovingly to Anita. Two days later Abuela Ana joined her husband, and together they lovingly live in the light of the universe. My dear Anita's heart was saddened, yet still over-filled with love and happiness for her Abuela Ana. Although she could not see her, Anita could feel Abuela Ana's love and protective powers softly flow through and around her. A few days later, Anita had to go on a business trip, and on her late-night flight home, there were problems with the plane upon take-off. The plane shook, vibrated, made loud clanging sounds, and smoke began to drift steadily throughout the plane. Most everyone feared that the plane would crash. Anita was seated in the emergency aisle of the plane when the captain came out of the cockpit. Not too far from her feet, on the floor, was a small trapdoor that he opened. He was manually inspecting the landing gear to determine its status of safety. Silently and without expression, he closed the trapdoor and returned to the cockpit. A man seated next to dear Anita made the comment to her that they were all going to die in an explosive crash. My dear Anita calmly said to him, "I am an aviation attorney. Have you ever heard of an aviation attorney dying in a plane crash? We don't die in plane crashes!" A few moments later the plane began to ascend higher into the air, then slowed and began to descend, over a lake, without the sound of one of its engines. Large amounts of fluid began pouring from the plane. The pilot was releasing all the fuel! The lights went out in the plane. Screams and prayers turned to be the course of action for the passengers. Not for Anita, though, for she was too familiar with plane engines and landing gears and herself to be fearful of death. She envisioned the safe landing of the plane on a foamed runway surrounded by firetrucks and ambulances (which she knew would not be needed). Unruffled and with inner peace, she looked out the side passenger window to the calm, perfectly clear sky of the night. A single shiny, bright yellow star was beaming light onto dear Anita's face. As the beauty of the star's shimmers twinkled in her thoughts, my dear Anita felt the powerfulness of her Abuela Ana's love enter her eyes and through her whole body. Abuela Ana was there! There in the night's sky as she said she would be! My dear Anita and her Abuela Ana were together once more! Forever together! All within the universe is one. The energy passes on like Abuela Ana, but it never ends. It simply takes on another bright form. And like Abuela Ana, it has the power to travel the universe, faster than the speed of light, to relay its meaning and oneness with another. Simply beautiful, don't you think? I do!

The plane safely landed on a foamed runway. It was discovered that like the Spantax Flight 995 accident, it was a recapped tread on a tire flying into the engine that caused the near disaster. The quick, professional thinking of the pilot to follow through with the take-off and empty the fuel before returning to the airport allowed the plane to remain intact with all passengers and crew remaining alive.

Remember how we have made references to synchrodestiny? It was during the Chopra seminars' discussions of universal awareness and how it connects with events and people in one's life that affirmed and amplified Anita's own beliefs of being at the right place at the right time were for a reason and that there were no accidents. Everything that happens in one's life is meant to be. There is no right or wrong— only lessons to be learned. As dear Anita mentioned earlier, "I have lucky days. Whatever happens is lucky. Even if bad should happen, it's lucky because it gives me something to study." As a forever student of the universe, Anita is always ready to learn the lessons of that which is presented to her. My dear Anita is always ready for lessons! How else can one account for all her accomplishments (honor student, loving daughter and granddaughter, aerobics instructor, cha-cha-cha dancer, pilot, aviation attorney just to name few!) Many times different people have told her that she is Just Too Much! Too Much Thinking! Too Much Dancing! Too Much Energy! Too Much Everything! Anita is just Too A-OK, if you will, with their Too Much beliefs of her. In her laughing, loving heart, she knows that all her Too Much has been synchrodestiny in motion for her. Everything that she is Too Much of is because the universe opened up to her at the right time and right place. Everything aligned perfectly for her. Perfectly, though, does not mean necessarily with perfect smoothness. There may be a few stones on the pathway, but these stones make us stronger as we step forward in our life. Think when Anita was at Dowling College preparing for medical school and Ronnie the Doctor wanted more from her than friendship. Anita knew that it was time to walk a new path and change her lesson plan. She left medical school and went out into the world on her own and met new people and learned various life lessons. These people and life lessons created her pathway to law school. Upon graduation time, her friend Larry was declined a law position because he did not have pilot skills. Anita, who had been a pilot, interviewed for the law position and was hired the same day. This is synchrodestiny in motion. Now that doesn't mean at the given time when things were aligning for her that she was aware of the fact. This in itself was another lesson that Anita learned. Dear Anita intuitively knew, though, to let life be and to become totally enrolled in and complete in full (with honors!) the lesson plans of life presented to her! The only Too Much that dear Anita never had was Too Much Nothing because EVERYTHING is always near her!

Synchrodestiny even took place during the Chopra seminar of Summoning of the Sacred, where the discussion of archetypes and mystic paths that merge within one's life was presented. For it was here that she met the presenter of the seminar, Dr. Jean Houston. Anita was seated in the front row listening and taking notes of Dr. Houston's words. Unbeknownst to Anita, Dr. Houston was taking mental notes of Anita. After the seminar, Anita got up and proceeded to exit the room, when she heard a female voice call out the words—you are a dragon. Anita turned around and saw Dr. Houston walking behind her. Once more, Dr. Houston called out the words—you are a dragon. Anita smiled, lightly laughed, turned her head slightly sideways in thought, absorbed what had just been spoken to her, and formulated her questions. "What made you think of dragons? Why would you think I am a dragon? What do you know of dragons? Are dragons a part of your life?"

Dr. Houston responded, "I don't think, I know you are a dragon. I observed you from the podium. Your hand movements, posture, choice of words, and the way you carry yourself tells me you are a dragon." Anita mentioned that she had been born in the year of the dragon and always had a fondness for dragons in her heart due to their truths and strengths. Anita also happened to be wearing one of the dragon rings her father had made for her. She showed it proudly to Dr. Houston, telling her that her father had made many pieces of jewelry for her in shapes of dragons and hearts and that the love of dragons had always been with her. Dr. Houston responded, in a jovial, yet matter-of-fact manner, that a dragon was an archetype for Anita to bring to life.

Archetype. Dragon. These two words kept spinning in Anita's mind for several days. Finally, she decided to call Dr. Houston to discuss further. Dr. Houston invited Anita to come to one of her salon small group mentoring programs being held at her home so they could explore for her the universal world where everything is in a state of possibility until it is perceived (allowing for the possibility to become reality). Anita flew to Dr. Houston's home in Oregon, where she was met by Dr. Houston and the other attendees of the salon. What a wonderful time Anita had! It was not at all what she was expecting, but that was fine with her. The universe is always filled with pleasant surprises for my dear Anita! She and the other attendees had a lot of hard work to do, but they also had lots of fun! One part of the salon program was to put on a play about the Wizard of Oz. Dear Anita was the Cowardly Lion—the before and after picture! All the characters in the play had to write their lines and perform in front of an audience of about 300 people. No small feat! The evening before the play, dear Anita stayed up during the night to write her own script. She wanted it to be touching and funny! The next morning, there was no time for rehearsal. The show was instant and live! All the characters from the Wizard of Oz (including little Toto) got on stage and began their performances. Anita was prepared with her own props, which allowed her to look and feel like the Cowardly Lion. She wore a beautiful angora wool tiger print (yes, tiger print—lions don't have any spots or stripes, and Anita loves color and prints of all kinds!) scarf that she whirled around her neck and let hang to the floor. She teased her thick hair up and out from her face like a lion's mane. She held her hands stretched out and wide to look like lion paws. When other characters were speaking, she was to appear meek and frightened. She did this by slightly bending downward and shaking her body, keeping her eyes low to the ground, and making soft whimpering sounds. But when it was time for her to give her lines as the lion, Anita transformed herself into energies of compassion and strength. Her posture became perfect in alignment with the ground. Her eyes moved up and opened wide in which to see all that was around. She took her hands (lion paws) and spread them even further apart and scratched at the sky (as if awakening not only herself, as the lion, but the new universe that surrounded her). Her voice became like that of a tenor's as she recited her lines of courage in a precious and distinct dictation of bravery. She conveyed that courage equals action and that one must not be frozen in fear, but must do what is necessary at the given time. She made lines light-hearted, too, so they could see that one should not be too serious. She told the audience a cute lion joke. "So, how do you brush a lion's teeth," asked Anita. "Very, very carefully," she answered. Both she and the audience roared! Laughter and fun—what a great time had by everyone! Laughter is fun and healthy and it can also be a shifter in reality! Think of a day where you had lots of laughter. Did your day not become suddenly more wonderful?! And if you can share your laughter, as dear Anita did as the Cowardly Lion, you can shift the reality of a whole room filled with people to having a more wonderful day!

Another exciting day of the salon for Anita was when all the attendees learned of Altered Perception (changing your past to a new present). One individual had a traumatic experience as a child that involved falling off the stage and badly hurting herself while performing. Her aunt was in the audience and screamed with terror at the incident. An ambulance had to be called. All her life, this woman could never forget that day and how the fall had changed her and her aunt's life in a negative manner. She felt guilty for having caused trauma to her body and aunt. In doing the Altered Perception she went back to the past and relived the event. In her mind of imagination, through the assistance of breathing and mantras, she rewrote the fall to be so minor that she simply brushed herself off and returned to the stage to complete her performance. She saw her aunt laughing and applauding with joy at the end of the show. Together they left and had a nice meal and talked about the success of the performance. Not only was her present mind believing the new version, but so were the cells in her body (both the existing and new ones being formed). All trauma from the fall had been released from her. Now, remember how we are one with everything in the universe? The woman in changing her past had also included her aunt in re-writing the past. She called her aunt to discuss the fall and now her aunt's, at the same time the woman's view changed, perception was automatically in sync with the present version of the fall. The aunt, too, had no remaining trauma. On the science side of things, this occurrence is tied in with quantum physics where we are all part of one another and the universe. Where there is a change in one (the woman), there will be a change in another (the aunt) simultaneously.

Altered Perception is a way to use your imagination to create reality. Another person of this program was a man who had always wanted to be a rabbi but told himself many years before that he could never be a rabbi due to being gay. He had studied for years the teaching of a rabbi on his own. He had purchased the clothes and various religious items a rabbi would use within his congregation. During the salon program, the man went through full motions of believing he was a rabbi in full dress, style, mannerism, reading, and use of religious items. The other attendees played the role of being members of his congregation. Like the previous tale of the woman, it completely transformed his perception of being a rabbi. He changed his self-made barriers of being gay and unwanted as a rabbi to be a successful and much-loved rabbi. His reality changed for the positive. He gave away his old thoughts and began rabbinical studies. Today he is a prestigious rabbi with a loving congregation.

My dear Anita found all these happy ending events to be magnificent and held them close to her heart. Anita, herself, had no events in her past that she wished to change. Not necessary, because all had been perfect for her, but because at the time the events were happening in her life, she remained calm, in awe, and always proceeded forward with a positive attitude. There were three times, as a baby and child, that Anita almost died. The first time, while living in Cuba, she was floating in an inner tube in the ocean, and she leaned over and tumbled headfirst in the salty water. With her eyes open she saw bubbles coming from her eyes going around her body to the top of the water. Anita's father's loving, watchful eye had been on her, and within a flash of a moment, he had swum to her side, grabbed her feet, and lifted her in the sky. She didn't cry, though, because she was too fascinated by the bubbles. The second time, while visiting in Cuba, Anita was on a ferry with her mother and father (and about ten other passengers). The boat began to take on water. Anita's father was a strong swimmer, and unfortunately, her mother did not know how to swim. As the ferry was slowly sinking into the sea, Anita's mother told her husband to please take Anita and swim to shore. How selfless and beautiful was her love for her daughter. Anita's mother was willing to die to ensure her daughter's safety. Anita's heart beats with love, gratitude, and admiration for her mother's love of self-sacrifice. Fortunately, before the ship went down, a rescue boat came and retrieved them to safety. The third time, in the United States, Anita was on the top of a high-dive diving board. She had gone up there not to dive, but to see what the pool looked like from that high of a distance. Out of nowhere a young boy came from behind and pushed her off. Not missing a beat, Anita took a bird's-eye view of all that was around her as she plunged to the water. No fear. Just wonderment (in the view and as to what had just happened). She slammed into the water and it felt like the stings of a million ants all over her body. She had her eyes open and again saw all the bubbles, which continued to fascinate her. The pool lifeguard had seen what had happened and rescued her from the pool (for which Anita is forever grateful). Minutes later she was back in the pool swimming! All three of these events could have been considered by some as traumatic and cause drama to unfold at the given time or in the future. Not in Anita's perception, though. She took the events to be just that—events in her life. She didn't allow herself to view them as negative, disturbing, or scarring of body or soul type happenings. She only saw the beauty of the events. The different sized bubbles from her eyes, the view from the sky as falling, and the abundant love her mother and father bestowed upon her were all events of beauty to her. Love, happiness, and wonderment have always encircled my dear Anita!

During the time she worked with Dr. Houston, dear Anita began to focus on her dreams. Dr. Houston had instructed her to leave a pen and open writing pad on her bedside table. As soon as she awoke, whether in the middle of the night or the morning, she should begin writing words of what she had dreamt. Anita had some pretty amazing dreams that would bring introductions to her future. One of the first dreams she wrote about was where she wandering in a field, looking for the right pasture. She continued to move from field to field, all of which were lush and green, but none felt to contain the pasture that her inner self was seeking to acquire. In her awakened state, as you know Anita was in a period of reflections of her life. This dream showed her that her life was beautiful (the fields), but that there must be another calling or service of gratitude (the right pasture) to explore. The seeds of harmony were being gently sown in the pasture that dear Anita would soon find. A majestic pasture of benevolence it would soon prove to be for Anita.

Another dream Anita had was that of a silver, shiny key. In her dream, she did not know where to put it. She could feel happiness being released from the key to her. She didn't want to let go of the key but knew she needed to put it somewhere for safekeeping. As she was trying to decide on the perfect spot, the key began to slowly grow in size. Suddenly, a huge door with a keyhole was in front of her. She took the key and placed it in the lock. As she turned the key, the door opened and the sun's rays of bright yellow shined upon her. She turned herself in spirals so that the sun could surround her from all sides and then Anita sat in seiza and smiled outside and inside of herself while the sun's light bathed her body in peace and happiness. Anita's senses told her that the key was from her father. Mr. Arango was protecting her and guiding her to opening the correct door to her future pasture of benevolence. Upon awakening, Anita's heart was embraced by the love of her father, which gave her much joy and enthusiasm in all that was blooming in her soon-to-be discovered pasture.

At one time, my dear Anita had a sweet little ferret named Bubbles. He came into her life when he was a sickly little hob. Anita nursed him back to a healthy and happy life. How Anita loved little Bubbles! She designed and created a beautiful outdoor dwelling for him. He had the freedom of a large space to run, climb, and burrow. While in the house he could explore and have his meals. He also had his own little train that he'd get in and travel by way of indoor railroad tracks to various destinations in the house. People would come over to the house to talk with Anita, and they would hear the choo-chooing of a train and think it was from some distance outside. Next thing they knew here Bubbles would come around the track to greet them and then off he'd go into his land of adventure! As a treat, Anita would feed him jelly and a banana slice. He would eat the jelly from her finger and go hide the banana slice for a later snack. At the end of the day, Anita would find his banana slice and remove it (due to it having gone bad). Animals have a wonderful way of teaching us things. Little Bubbles taught Anita how to be joyfully in the moment of all that is happening (to include the events, people, and loving animals).

One night Bubbles came to Anita in a dream. She was walking him on a leash, and he was smelling the people and situations they encountered during their walk, allowing him to make royal and firm decisions. Bubbles would communicate what was taking place to Anita. Upon awakening, Anita realized from the Bubbles dream, that one's consciousness is awake as we sleep to reveal secrets to our life. We must listen to our dreams for the secrets to unfold and become a positive energy in the creation of our future reality.

My dear Anita became more and more inquisitive regarding her dreams. She reached out to a Houston psychologist (PhD) for additional clarity regarding the events and symbolisms in her dreams. It is a rather humorous tale of when they first met. My dear Anita was wearing her favorite ruby red suede boots that come almost to her knees. On the drive to her appointment, it began to rain in a downpour. She did not want her boots (or herself) to get wet, so she grabbed an umbrella quickly from the back seat of her car and proceeded to the building. The doctor met her at the door and stared at her in disbelief. Kiddingly he said, "So this is how you dress to see a psychologist? Bright red boots and holding a Mary Poppins umbrella? Let me get my notepad to make notes!" They both laughed in fun and jest. You see, dear Anita had gone to see the play *Mary Poppins* a few evenings before, and purchased, as a keepsake of the evening, a Mary Poppins umbrella (to include the colorful parrot head handle). Needless to say, dear Anita created a very good rapport with the psychologist. She was most grateful for his kindness and knowledge regarding the interpretations of her dreams. My dear Anita's kindness grew stronger toward him. He was diagnosed with cancer and had fears regarding his illness and the possibility of death. Dear Anita became his Chinese doctor and offered her own friendly advice. She discussed his fears with him and made him her famous green soup (made from organic celery, curly parsley, zucchini, and green beans) to bring his pH balance in perfect alignment with his body. She used Feng Shui to give his office and himself organization and structure. His fears and outlook on his health became more peaceful, healthy, and at one. My dear Anita holds fond memories of this kind man!

My dear Anita during this time was continuing her lessons with Dr. Houston remotely. They would talk once a week, on Wednesday, for an hour to review all that was happening in Anita's reflections of her life, growth, and quest for her majestic pasture. Dr. Houston mentioned to Anita that she was a powerful Frequency Orchestrator. Anita with a laugh and smile replied that she was happy to be powerful, but to please explain what was meant by the term Frequency Orchestrator?

Dr. Houston stated to Anita that she had the gift of being able to change the frequency of energy within others. Your energies of joy, happiness, and enthusiasm begin to enter the room as you cross its threshold. You are movement of energy in motion! It goes from your heart to their heart without even a word being said. People feel your energy both on the inside and outside. Anita loved hearing this, not for her ego to hear, but for her inner compassionate warrior to hear, so she may be able to serve others with more mastery of knowledge and skill in the benevolent pasture that was awaiting her arrival.

One Wednesday, before Anita was to hold her weekly telephone conference with Dr. Houston, she learned that her mother, Angelina, had been sped away to the hospital in an ambulance. Earlier that morning, Angelina had taken her little dog for a walk. Her mother has always had love and protection for others in her heart. While walking her little dog, she saw a pit bull dart madly across the street to her direction. Without thinking, she intuitively picked the little dog up and put her in her jacket. The pit bull jumped on Angelina and tumbled her face down to the ground. The pit bull mauled Angelina's arms in trying to get to the little dog. Angelina kept her arm and body in a position so as the little dog would remain safe. Neighbors came out when they heard all the noise that was being created due to the attack. They pulled the pit bull away and saw blood coming from the tears in Angelina's jacket. The neighbors sent her by ambulance to the hospital. While at the hospital it was determined that Angelina needed immediate heart surgery due to their diagnosis of the main artery being clogged. At the beginning of her phone conference with Dr. Houston, Anita told her about her mother's status. She told Dr. Houston that she did not feel her mother really needed surgery and that it was the trauma of the pit bull attack that had increased her blood pressure and caused the physicians to think there was a blockage in her arteries. Anita and Dr. Houston discussed remote healing for Angelina. Both were in agreement that Anita should use the steps of remote healing to prevent Angelina from having unnecessary surgery.

My dear Anita began the remote healing. She went inside herself and became calm and at one with all that was around her. She used her energies of love to take her on a flight, as a healing dragon, from her home in Houston to the hospital in New York. Once she arrived in her mother's hospital room, she saw her mother lying on the bed resting comfortably. She also saw all the various medical equipment in the room making sounds and recording her mother's heartbeat, pulse, and blood pressure. Anita made herself become as small as a grain of rice as she swiftly penetrated through the skin above her mother's heart. She then penetrated and entered the arteries leading into Angelina's heart. She began to scrub the inside of the arteries, allowing the flow of blood to effortlessly move through them and into the heart. Once done, Anita exited and returned to her mother's hospital room. Her mother was in a deep, restful sleep. Anita smiled and sent her healing powers of love. Then she flew back to Houston. Once back, she called the hospital and was told that her mother was doing very well and that her blood pressure had returned back to a normal, healthy range. No surgery needed to be done. Anita rejoiced. Anita never told her mother of the remote healing. This was the way Anita wanted it to be. Anita, for a brief moment, had become her mother on the ferry while her mother became her. The only thing of importance to Anita was that her mother be protected and saved from any harm. Anita's mother left the hospital that night and returned home to her little dog, who welcomed her with soft barks of *I love you*. Angelina picked the little dog up and gave her a big hug and told her that she loved her too. By the way, the little dog's name is Anita. She was named after my dear Anita! Needless to say, my dear Anita's love abounds everywhere in all different shapes, beings, and styles!

Not too long after the remote healing, dear Anita had a dream of a polar bear. This was a huge white polar bear whose name was Su (the sound made by the creation of the universe). His whiteness reminded her of the Crown chakra, which is a brilliant white. Su entered Anita's dream by standing on his two hind legs and walking into her room. He was somewhere between nine and ten feet tall. He was snow white with charcoal-black eyes. Anita was mesmerized by his immense beauty. Although Su was fierce-looking at first, Anita remained calm and had questions for him. "Polar Bear, why have you come?" asked Anita.

"To see if you are worthy. To remind you that if you have any fear, you must release it, because fear can prevent the free flow of energy," replied Su.

"Polar Bear, why do you have such large claws?" asked Anita.

"To be able to dig deep within me for answers to the purpose of my life," replied Su.

"Polar Bear, why are your eyes black?" asked Anita.

"So I may see inside the soul," replied Su.

Su came closer and closer to her with each answer. Soon he was directly before her. He began to smell the air surrounding her and then proceeded to smell her from the tips of her toes to the top of her head. He pulled back slightly so he could look directly into Anita's eyes. His charcoal-black eyes connected with her chocolate-brown eyes, and with his spiritual thoughts he shared a few of his universal wisdoms. Intuitively and lovingly Su said, "Anita, you must use energy and strength wisely and conserve them in pursuit of your true goals and benevolent pasture. The color white is the purity of the spirit. Fearless universal energy flows effortlessly when fear is 100 percent absent. I am your ally in getting past any hidden fears you may have. Also, I am your awakening and your honor-bound guardian. I love you, dear Anita, and I will always only be a thought away." Without letting go of her sight, Su slowly moved backward, on all four legs, leaving the room and Anita's dream.

Upon awakening, my dear Anita was full of energy, and she immediately began to research polar bears. She discovered that they are the most powerful predators and fearless animals and they have inner strengths to overcome adversities within their environment of the Arctic Circle. Anita further discovered that polar bears symbolize purity, rebirth, transformation, creatures of dreams, and desirable ally spirit helpers. Anita felt Su's love dancing in her heart. She knew that this dance in her heart was movement in the right direction to her highly sought-after pasture. Anita was confident that it was only a matter of time before more answers would be coming her way.

Dear Anita spoke to Dr. Houston about Su. Dr. Houston informed her that Su was one of her archetypes. Archetypes seek you out and give you a stronger purpose; archetypes are energies that can support and guide you toward actualizing your dreams. In Anita's mind, she was realizing that the archetype of Su must be connected with the archetype of Dragon. "Dr. Houston, tell me about Dragon. I want to know about Dragon," stated Anita.

"At this time, all there is to tell you is that Dragon is with you. He has already introduced himself to you twice. Think back of the times you were a little, little girl. You will recognize his introductions within your childhood memory. Once you remember, let me know and I will show you the path so you may go to him. He is waiting for you with both the patience of a parent and the extreme excitement of a little boy.

"There is also one more archetype destined for you, and this is Kuan Yin. She has touched you several times without you being aware of who she was, yet each time you felt her love within your heart. She has been introduced to you by another who held you in honor and truth. Kuan Yin came to you out of love and respect for who you are and what you have done unselfishly for others. She rests serenely within your home. You must look for her. She is 'The Promise' in your future!"

Chapter 13

Kannon Anita

The Promise

In my mind's eye, I can see my beautiful dear Anita dressed all in white, seated in seiza at the top of her staircase in front of Kuan Yin as the lit candles' beams dance lovingly in the calmness of the moon's glow. I can feel Anita's energies of love, kindness, and compassion as she says her prayers.

Aad guray nameh
jugaad guray nameh
Sat guray nameh
siree guroo day-ay nameh

(I bow to the Primal Power
I bow to the all-encompassing Power and Energy
I bow through that which God creates
I bow to the creative Power.)

As my dear Anita says the first line to the prayer, her hands are in prayer position resting near her heart. As she says the second line, she raises her hands up high to be nearer to Kuan Yin's heart. On the third line, she returns her hands to her heart. Lastly, on the fourth line, she raises her hands once more toward Kuan Yin's heart. The bond of love between Kuan Yin and Anita is inseparable. For they are one.

My dear Anita gets up early to say her prayers. Her day starts with the peace found in the moon and the radiance of the stars that nestle around her as she prays to Kuan Yin. And as she finishes her prayers, the moon and stars remain within her body, and the sun begins to awaken and shine brilliantly upon her soul, revealing to her, in a snuggling manner, that a new day of knowledge through adventure and excitement awaits her in the universe's safe hands of love.

Please let me tell you of Kuan Yin. Glorious is she! She is the Goddess of Mercy and Compassion. Hers was not an easy life. Kuan Yin knew much about suffering. She was born in China to a father who was cruel and wanted her to marry a man of great wealth. The man, though, was uncaring to her and others. Kuan Yin pleaded with her father to let her join a temple and become a nun. Her father reluctantly agreed. He instructed the monks to make her life as unpleasant as possible. She was given tasks and chores to complete that were never-ending. She worked day and night as others did nothing. She never lost her heart of love and compassion. Kuan Yin's father became very ill and there was little hope for his recovery. At last, his shaman pronounced that his life could be saved if they could find someone who had never held hate in their heart and if that someone agreed to cut off their two arms as the ultimate sacrifice to bring health and life back to another person. The shaman only knew of one such person and that was Kuan Yin. When presented with the proposal, Kuan Yin's compassion and love, for all and everything, were so great that she forgave her father for the atrocities he had inflicted upon her and allowed her arms to be severed in order to save his life. At the time of her own death, as she was ascending to heaven, she relinquished nirvana and asked to be returned to Earth so she may continue to help those in need until all suffering from the world was gone. Her name, Kuan Yin, translates to the one who hears the cries of the world's sufferings.

Now, according to Indian beliefs, Kuan Yin was originally Avalokita (or Avalokitesvara). Avalokita was depicted as a man (sometimes as a woman or even genderless). Like Kuan Yin, Avalokita was full of compassion for others' suffering and did all he could to help. It is said that he became so overwhelmed that he broke into a thousand pieces. He was put back together by Amithaba Buddha and given a total of eleven heads and a thousand arms (with an eye in each hand of each arm), thus allowing him to help others by the multitudes.

Kuan Yin is also known as Kannon in Japan. Kannon personifies compassion and is worshiped by most everyone in Japan. Statues of her are present in most temples throughout Japan. As a matter of fact, Anita, when in Japan as Mr. Tanaka's guest, visited Sanjusangendo. This temple was built in honor of Kannon in the twelfth century. It houses a thousand and one statues of Kannon. It is a beautiful and breathtaking temple. Kannon also through her mercy and compassion is not only a deity for helping human suffering, but for animals (including beloved pets like dogs and cats) as well. Her heart has no boundaries for those suffering or in need of protection.

My dear Anita had been touched several times by Kannon's love and did not realize it, per se. Of course, please keep in mind that dear Anita is always sending and receiving love at all times (for it is part of her high energy). Although she may not have been aware at the time of Kannon's love for her, Anita was aware of having received love. At

Sanjusangendo, Anita could feel love and compassion surrounding her as she toured the temple. The beauty of Kannon and her love and kindness to others brought quick, small tears of joy to Anita's eyes. Anita, with her compassionate warrior path of life, could relate so strongly to Kannon's honorable qualities. Many years later, Mr. Tanaka, after having studied to become a Christian man of God, left all his worldly goods to Anita. He purposely came to her home when she was not there and left her everything. Anita was the one person he held to be most of honor and truth. In the belongings he had bequeathed her was a statuette of a beautiful Japanese woman, serenely sitting as if ending her prayers, in a white kimono (with tan etchings of style), holding a small, covered vessel within her delicate yet all-knowing right hand, while her left hand, of smooth, long fingers, rests calmly across her legs. Her face, slightly tilted to the left, as if releasing thoughts of compassion's wisdom to the world, smiles a gracious and giving-of-love smile. When you look at her, you can feel the love entering your heart. This, my friends, is Kannon!

For Kannon to enter your world, she must be brought to you. Anita's beloved friend Mr. Tanaka had brought Kannon to her. Anita, from the very first day of having received Kannon, was enchanted by her mystique and beauty. Kannon arrived, entrusted to Anita, encased in a glass display box where you can see her body, mind, and soul from every angle. Dear Anita has her divinely residing atop an older wooden desk, which was Mr. Tanaka's as well, at the top of her staircase, in an area of honor and prominence. Anita lights candles every day as her gift of love and esteem for Kannon. Anita presents fresh-cut flowers, as well, in her honor. These flowers long outlive the other fresh-cut flowers Anita places around her home. Love lives with love.

Over the years, Anita has acquired nine Kannons (or Kuan Yins if you would like) and they are all living lovingly throughout her home and the Aikido dojo! Yes, Kannon is in the dojo for all the Aikido students to honor and admire. As you will learn, Aikido is a path of compassion, and as you know Kannon is the Goddess of Mercy. She is also known as Izunomi O'kami, the Aikido Goddess of Compassion.

Except for two Kannons, all were gifts to dear Anita. The reason why I mention this is because there is a fascinating story regarding the two Kannons that Anita purchased. Actually, she only made one purchase, but she received two paintings. Anita had been at the Chopra seminar and noticed a painting of a woman with an illuminating aura, dressed in a long, free-flowing white gown and riding on top of a dragon that was venturing through the waves of an ocean, as a bright star gave light for their journey. In her hands, the woman holds a twig from a tree and a small bottle. As fate would have it, or should I say synchrodestiny, the artist was also at the seminar. Anita fell in love with the painting, instantly, and purchased it. She requested that the artist have it shipped to her home. When it arrived it proved to be the incorrect painting. The painting that arrived was one that Anita found to be unsettling. This painting depicted an individual who may be a man or woman seated on what appears to be a hard surface and wearing red and green clothing that is not free-flowing, but more attached to the body. The background of the painting reflects an encasing wall of stone. This painting was the complete opposite of what she had seen and requested to be shipped to her. The first painting represented beauty, freedom, love, and a journey into a new life. The second painting was more representative of ambiguity, stagnation, and no journey to be explored. Anita did not want this painting and called the artist. He apologized and stated he would send the correct painting and that Anita may return the one received. Within a couple of days, the new painting arrived and Anita's heart began to glow. She could feel all the love and truths meant to be in this the correct painting. The delivery service did not take back the incorrect painting, though. Anita called the artist several times and left messages but he did not reply. This is how Anita came to have two paintings with one purchase! Anita realized that the unsettling painting was meant to be hers. In the back of her mind, she knew there must be a reason why she was made the owner of this painting. She also knew that, for now, she did not want it to be near her. She had it placed in the ladies' dressing room of the dojo (the farthest spot possible from her). As time passed, Anita changed her feeling from unsettling to love for the painting. It now has found a new place inside of Anita's home. It hangs near the picture of Anita's Abuela Ana and the tormented Jesus bust. If you ask me, I believe that the two paintings, which Anita purchased as one, represent the meaning of Yin and Yang. You must have the opposite of one to appreciate and be aware of the other. And all, no matter what, will be surrounded by love.

Now I feel confident that you have come to realize that the original painting that Anita fell in love with was Kannon. To tell a little bit more about Kannon, she is usually depicted as carrying a twig of a tree and a small bottle (just like in the painting Anita purchased) and riding a dragon. These three things represent the spirit of Kannon's compassionate soul. The small bottle contains her wisdom, which she graciously shares with others. The twig of the tree serves two purposes. First, it is the twig of a weeping willow tree, which allows her to evenly sprinkle the wisdom of compassion from her bottle upon those in need. Also, the weeping willow twig allows her to freely weep her tears (much like the blowing of the wind allows the weeping willow branches to be in motion). Her tears, like that of a compassionate warrior, are a way of cleansing one's soul. Kannon's tears of compassion clean the pains and injustices that exist. With love's purity in her tears and heart, she is able to remove suffering from the world.

Kannon is also the patroness and protector of fishermen (and all who may need protection), and this is where I, as Dragon, come into the painting. We dragons are very strong both physically and mentally and full of courage. We have great knowledge of the world's spirituality, for it lives within our own spirituality. We give guidance to others by bestowing our courage upon them as Kannon leads them safely away from any type of possible discord that may be floating in their seas of life. We love Kannon and we love to feel her energy as she rides upon our backs over the waves of the oceans. Her warmth of goodness and love travels to our spine and throughout our bodies. She emphasizes our strength with her compassion and spirituality. Dear Anita said to me once that she can sit for hours in seiza and meditate and never grow tired. That is how it is with Kannon and me when we are at sea. We can travel over the waves slowly or at lightning speed to ensure all remain out of harm's way. To see her heart reach out to the seamen in their boats and give them peace and protection is unfathomable beauty to me. Of course, my dear Anita did the same, did she not, with the lost souls from the *Ocean Ranger*? My heart beats joyously and my mind opens wide as I think of my dear Anita's love for others. Kannon and Anita are the same to me. So much love and so much beauty!

Once, after I had taken Kannon across the Pacific Ocean and back to Japan, Kannon left me so she could help those who were suffering high in the mountains. I had the remainder of the day to myself, so I decided to partake in the Saigoku Kannon Pilgrimage and find a nice relaxing spot to meditate. Yes, we dragons do meditate! The pilgrimage consists of thirty-three temples dedicated to Kannon. Being a dragon I can remain invisible to others, if I desire, and travel effortlessly and timelessly wherever I choose. Which is a good thing, because this is a 1,500-mile pilgrimage that spans Japan's east and west coasts! Thirty-three temples in honor of Kannon! Isn't that wonderful? The love for her is all throughout the land and spirit of Japan. On the pilgrimage, I especially enjoyed visiting the Nanendo Temple because it was the ninth temple on the pilgrimage. I keep Anita close to my heart at all times and I know how she loves the number nine. And of course, visiting the Rukkakudo Temple is very special to me, as well, because it is the eighteenth temple on the pilgrimage and it makes me think of Kannon. You see, the eighteenth day of every month is Kannon's Ennichi (holy day). Which, again, makes me think of my dear Anita. Anita loves to celebrate the eighteenth of every month! She adorns Kannon with flowers of vibrant colors and lights candles (which stay lit throughout the day) and ensures that all nine Kannons within her home are represented. She also says additional prayers to include:

Goddess of the Cleansing Power
Purify me this sacred hour
Banish doubt, disease, fear, and anxiety
Fill me with love, gratitude, compassion, kindness, and courage
Izunomomi O'Kami.

and

Ong Namo guru dayv namo

(I bow to the subtle divine wisdom, the divine wisdom within).

As she prays, Anita holds her Kannon 108 prayer beads and repeats one of Kannon's favorite prayers 108 times. All the while Anita remains focused on the twin flame soul's pure love of compassion that she and Kannon share.

As you know, all days are lucky for dear Anita, but she holds the eighteenth as especially lucky days due to her love for Kannon. Plus, for Anita, if you add the one and eight from eighteen, you get nine. Again, my dear Anita's favorite number is nine. She thinks nines are fabulous! How she makes me smile with her number nines! She will proudly tell you that when growing up she lived on 108 63rd Street. You guessed it! One plus zero plus eight equals nine! Six plus three equals nine! Then add those two nines and you get eighteen. Add the one and eight and you get nine, again! In her passion for the number nine, she intertwines a regal state of honesty and little girl playfulness! Much love to you, my dear, sweet Anita!

During the pilgrimage, I was able to locate a magnificent place to meditate. It was in the forest of the Kegon-ji Temple, where a Kannon statue stood gracefully amongst the trees. In the background, I could hear the unique sounds of all the crickets chirping. As I was preparing to meditate, I saw a beautiful baby bluebird softly land and flutter gingerly on Kannon's sleeve. The baby bird must have just learned how to fly. He slowly marched, at his own pace, with an expression of humbleness and pride in his eyes toward Kannon's hand. His wings were spread out, like a little warrior ready to be of service and take flight when needed. He made no sound, but within his beak, I could see a tiny twig. He dropped the tiny twig in Kannon's hand as if he was saying to her, "Please, let me help you. I am here for you." In the wind, I could hear Kannon's voice softly say, "Oh my dear beloved friend, thank you for being here with me. Yes, let's go together and help those who need us." Next, I saw the baby bluebird gallantly lift its wings in flight, as if it had flown a thousand times before, and fly toward the heavens as the spirit of Kannon flew beside him. Love empowers love.

This is an excellent time to discuss with you Kannon's love for children. Kannon is a guardian of women. In her guardianship, she will bless women who may have difficulty conceiving with a robust daughter or son. She will surround the mother and child with love and excellent health. Kannon will give the child a mind filled with infinite libraries to hold and retrieve the great wonders of the world and the free will to do as they so choose with their knowledge. Kannon is not one to control another's life, whether a child or adult, for she knows one's life must be governed by their own consciousness, but she will always be near to lovingly guide in the protection of their overall well-being.

Having been born on Valentine's Day, my dear Anita has always been one to love and be loved. Her whole life has been filled with hearts and love. So much love can only attract more love. Truehearted love such as Anita's and Kannon's is a spirit that is joyfully shared with innocence and honor from the heart's soul. As the spirit of love travels through the universe, it touches all within its path. The innocence in this spirit of love is that it asks for nothing in return. Its whole being is just to give happiness, wonderment, and protection. The honor of the spirit of love is to give respect, acknowledgment, and gratitude. The spirit of love needs no announcement nor fanfare as it travels to its destination. The heart's soul receiving the love knows in a moment's heartbeat that it has arrived. The warmth and jubilation of its arrival dances throughout the body and into every fiber and cell. The dance may be as fast-moving as the cha-cha or slower like the waltz! Everyone has their own rhythm of dance in celebration for the spirit of love. And what is a celebration? A gathering of friends and loved ones to have a time of happiness and enjoyment. The spirit of love that the heart's soul receives sends invitations of love to others to join in the celebration. The gathering happens in a moment's thought of love. The spirit of love dances in celebration with all forever.

The spirit of love can come at any time and any place. One morning, after having said her prayers to Kannon, dear Anita proceeded on with her morning. The sun had risen and it was time for exercise and yoga. On her yoga mat, as she was doing stretches, her mind was reaching out to the universe for knowledge on how to assist others in a manner that would benefit their health. In doing such, she moved directly to the hardwood floor to be closer to Earth. She wanted to feel

Earth's support upon her body for additional aligning and balancing of body and spirit. As she was moving from her hara, new techniques of stretching were beginning to happen. This was a special feeling for Anita. She was thinking that she had just discovered a new way of stretching and that she would call it "Earth Stretch."

Then suddenly she began crying. No, more of a sobbing. A sobbing from a place of knowingness. The sobbing became uncontrollable as her tears fell to the floor (to Earth). These were not tears of sadness, but tears of understanding of what had just happened. Kannon had come to her and given her the knowledge of the "Earth Stretch." Kannon, in her selflessness, had revealed to Anita stretching techniques to use with others to help ensure they remained protected in excellent health. Kannon had given a piece of her own creativity to my dear Anita. Kannon's love from her heart's soul had been blessed upon Anita. Anita's tears turned to joy! Anita, with her Kannon beads in hand, began to dance around the room with Kannon's spirit of love. As Anita continued to dance, with enchanting music dedicated to Kannon, she began to bow in her movements. As she bowed, Anita promised Kannon with great gratitude, over and over, that with Kannon's gift of creativity, she would always help others and would never allow her own ego to take credit. Anita could feel more of Kannon's spirit of love entering her heart's soul, and it soothingly spread through her body, giving healing energy and movement. Thank you, thank you, thank you was all Anita could say after pledging her promise. Anita's spirit of love from Kannon would soon be dancing with others in her universe of Aikido.

Chapter 14
The World of Dragons Anita

I Am. We Are. This Is Me.

My dear Anita looked so beautiful as she slept. Please let me reassure you that it is not my style to watch people sleep, but tonight was different from all the other nights that Anita had slept, for I was to make my formal introduction to her. Dr. Houston had previously informed Anita that she was a dragon and had met me twice before. In her heart and soul, Anita had always felt like a dragon and believed that there must be a dragon watching over her. She was confident that guardian angels may take on different forms, so for her it was only natural to have a guardian angel dragon! So wise is my dear Anita! Before falling asleep my dear Anita had asked the universe and her beloved Kannon to tell her of me, Aiki Dragon.

As you know, many, many times I have sailed the seas with Kannon to help her bring safety, compassion, love, and kindness to those in need. When Kannon relayed to me Anita's desire to learn of me, my heart rejoiced. I felt as though I had been tenderheartedly struck by Cupid's arrow. My heart filled larger with more love and benevolence.

My dear Anita was not a lost soul in need like so many of the others that Kannon and I had helped, but she was a gentle, loving soul who desired more knowledge of herself and those who surrounded her world.

Silently, I flew into my dear Anita's bedroom as she slept. Her beauty reminded me of Kannon's beauty and love. Dear Anita's head rested so serenely upon her pillows, and I could see lying on top of the bed linens above the area of her solar plexus chakra, her regal hands were softly moving their fingers in a spiraling open-and-close manner (the same way a dragon stretches their hands and fingers). With honor, I slowly moved toward Anita and leaned over and gently whispered in her ear (and mind's eye), "I am Aiki, Aiki Dragon, my dear sweet Anita. Oh, how wonderful it is to talk with you at last. I smile to you in gratitude and love for knowing that finally, I can share with you the mystical reality of my world. The World of Dragons. Please know that you are correct in believing that I am one of your guardian angels. I am one of your guides. And you, in turn, are a guardian angel of mine." Anita's bedroom was filled with a beautiful bright yellow light. It was the light of Abuela Ana's shining star, for she was in the room as well. Abuela Ana knew of me at the time of Anita's birth, and she was the one who granted me permission to enter Anita's bedroom as she lay sleeping.

My dear Anita, as her eyes remained closed, attentively replied, "My dear Aiki, yes, I know of you, for though I did not know your name, you have always lived with love in my heart. You were there when I played and sang songs with my little friend Selena. And you were there when I decided to go flying on my tricycle. My father introduced me to Confucius, which led me to the I-Ching. Now I am beginning to believe that you led me to the I-Ching, for it was around this time that dragons became so real within me. I have flown the skies in small planes with ease and at one with the universe. I must have had your wings near me then, my dear Aiki Dragon."

I answered, "My dear Anita, my wings and heart have been with you since birth, but it was not my wings that allowed you to fly. It was your own self-confidence, grace, and trust in the universe that allowed you to fly. You earned your own wings by your truths of courage, love, and compassion. Love abounds you.

"My dear Anita, it is through your love that we dragons request your assistance, as there is much work that needs to be done. You need to enlighten humans to the knowledge and existence of dragons. You are the chosen one to release the dragons back into the world of mankind. There is so much more for me to tell you, my dear Anita, but as you have grown to understand, time is not a reality and is irrelevant at this moment. I am returning to the Dragon Council to inform them of having been with you. They will be so delighted. I can already see smiles on their faces, brightness in their eyes, and the release of love's laughter in their hearts. Very soon, I will send two dragons to discuss with you the importance that you play in our future. And soon, my dear Anita, you will know how to visit us and be a part of the Dragon Council. Rest and sleep well, my dear Senorita Dragonsita. A whole new world of life and amazement is about to be revealed to you. A world that will greatly and joyously astound you. A world that will lead you to the benevolent pasture that you are seeking. And you have all the time you need, my dear Anita."

In the morning, my dear Anita remembered everything from my visit with her. Her day was busy with running errands, but through her mind, she kept hearing me say that I would be sending two dragons to her and that very soon she would know how to visit the Dragon Council. The dragon part of my dear Anita's mind went wild with energy! A trait that all dragons have! Our wild energy consists of being in the moment, playful, somewhat mischievous, and rambunctious with laughter! Lots of laughter! We love to laugh and make others laugh!

We feel that humans tend to be too serious from time to time and they need to lighten up and laugh more (alone and in groups with others). Humans need to tell more jokes! In fact, I have a joke for you now! Do you know why dragons are such great storytellers? Because they have exquisite tails! Heh-heh! My dear Anita once told me a wonderful joke. A man was driving through the country and when he gets to the top of a hill, he has a flat tire. The man removes the lug bolts and places them on the ground and they roll down the hill into the drain. He is at a loss as to what to do. He then hears a pssst. The man turns around and sees a man behind the fence of a psychiatric hospital. "Pssst, mister, why don't you take one lug bolt from each of the three tires and use them for the fourth." The man is amazed and commends the guy on such a brilliant idea and asks why he is in a psychiatric hospital. The guy responds, "Hey, I may be crazy, but I'm not stupid!" Isn't that a great joke! It also has a great sense of morality to it too. Never judge. Just because a person may have limited mental capabilities does not mean that they are incapable of great thoughts and good deeds! As you will learn dragons do not judge others. Nor do we judge ourselves. We are who we are and are very proud of the fact. We want all to take pride in being who they are and not judge themselves or others!

Later that day, in the late afternoon, dear Anita was sitting on her third-floor porch looking at two of the nine beautiful old live oak trees that surround her property. They are sort of like Yin and Yang trees. They are both approximately two hundred years old. Romantically, their limbs cross over to one another. Between the two of them is a small live oak that is approximately a hundred years old. Most certainly, it is their offspring. A happy little tree family! And these trees know love. Anita sends them (and all that is near) her love. The trees share the love by graciously inviting the birds, lizards, and squirrels to live in their branches. A very happy family, indeed! Dragons love all that is nature! Especially dragonflies! They fly in a grand manner with beauty soaring through their wings! A dragonfly is Nature's reminder to the world that dragons do exist!

As my dear Anita was sitting on the porch, I quietly nudged her with the breeze that was blowing between the live oaks. Anita felt a slight tingle in her heart, and her thoughts told her I was near. She then thought of the two dragons I had mentioned. As the thought was leaving her mind, my two dragon friends appeared before her. Remember, thought is power. Anita thought of me, which led to the thought of the two dragons. Thus, they became her reality. The universe always knows how to answer one's thoughts!

Now my two dragon friends are very formal individuals. They wear tuxedos everywhere they go! I have given them the nickname of Yin and Yang because they are so different and yet so much the same as the other. When dear Anita first saw them, it was as if she was seeing old friends. Love was everywhere! In her excitement, she started giggling like a little girl, which caused them to start giggling. Have you ever seen grown dragons giggle? It's quite a sight! Anita had turned them into giggling little kids! Soon the little kid giggles turned into grown-up laughter. Loud, fun, and boisterous dragon laughter! Yin was in a red tuxedo with a green cummerbund and bow tie while Yang was in a green tuxedo with a red cummerbund and bow tie. Anita loved their tuxedos! Yin and Yang could tell that Anita loved their tuxedos, so they playfully started doing a modeling show on the porch for her. Then Anita got up and pretended to model too! Soon, all of them were strutting the catwalk in laughter! I told you dragons have a great sense of humor! It is fun to be a dragon!

As the laughter slowed down, it was time for Yin and Yang to explain to Anita the reasons why they came to her. "Dear Anita," began Yin, "our beloved friend Aiki Dragon has asked us to join you this evening, so we may illuminate the significance of your importance to the World of Dragons. First, as Aiki Dragon told you last night, he is your guardian angel. He is your mentor and will always be with you and give you guidance in all that lies before you. Also, you have a predominant position in our world. Aiki Dragon, and all of the dragons, need you to be our spokesperson, or maybe I should say spokesdragon, for you are a hybrid of human and dragon. You are the chosen one to open the World of Dragons to mankind. Anita, we dragons are everywhere. Our frequency is such that humans cannot see us, but we are amongst you. We love you. We love the earth's nature and mankind. Through you, we want healing for mankind. Not healing in the sense of directly dissipating disease, but the healing of giving mankind the beauty and happiness of health by raising their spiritual consciousness through love, compassion, peace, dance, music, laughter, and the movements of Aikido. Aikido is the benevolent pasture for which you have been searching. The beauty of it is that you have been in this pasture of compassion and love for many years now, and it is growing with each and every movement you make within the dojo. Everything will only become better and better as you move within its sphere. Its sphere is housed within the Tao."

Yang began to talk. "In the near future, you need to write a book about your life and how it involves dragons. This will be a wonderful way to begin the introduction of dragons to the world. From there you must write children's books meant for all ages to read. Everyone is young at heart and filled with love and adventure. These books will include dragons, humans, nature, and those from otherworldly realms. When the time is right, Aiki Dragon will see to it that he is present in the writings and that you have the assistance needed to make everything come forth. Everything will be as it should be. Remember, the universe lovingly gives us what we ask for at the time it is needed. Synchrodestiny is always alive and moving forward in our worlds."

In unison, Yin and Yang harmoniously concluded in saying, "Thank you for allowing us to be your guests. It has been a wonderful evening, and we look forward to seeing you soon at the Dragon Council. We bid you a good evening and wish all the wisdom, joy, love, and happiness that has been blessed upon you to find its way to all mankind. We love you, dear Anita." Both Yin and Yang tugged at their bow ties and were instantly gone.

Anita smiled and giggled in glee. What a wonderful evening it had been with her dear friends. Their words were still sounding within her mind. Anita was thinking up questions about what had just been told to her. Once more, I had the breeze nudge my dear Anita. "Yes, Aiki, I know you are here. I am ready to be of service, to be a powerful, amplified, creative vehicle to help you, all the dragons and mankind," stated Anita.

I simply whispered, through the trees, "Thank you, my dear Anita." Tears were in my eyes of great gratitude for the most beautiful and compassionate warrior that I have the honor to call as "My Dear Anita."

The next day, dear Anita woke up in the early hours of the morning and immediately went to the gracefully poised porcelain Kannon figurine that Mr. Tanaka had given her. With tears of love and enthusiasm, Anita sat in seiza, lit a candle, bowed and prayed to Kannon, and asked her questions regarding Aiki Dragon and Yin and Yang's visits. Kannon's loving voice softly entered Anita's thoughts, saying, "You are much loved, my dear. Aiki Dragon and his friends, Yin and Yang, are in need of your soulful spirit of love and compassion to open the pathway of their World of the Dragons to all those on Earth. You are one of a pure heart who sends love to all that she sees. The dragons need your love and warrior strength to fly high so they may be seen and of assistance to all. As a loving, compassionate warrior, your service to the dragons will allow them to be of service to you and all the human world. Joyously be aware and listen to the feelings that you receive when you think of Aiki Dragon. These feelings come from his heart to yours, and they will manifest that which needs to be manifested. Anita, you are so insightful to your questions of everything and yet you have never questioned anything. Bravely and lovingly you always let all be as all is meant to be. With pleasure take Aiki Dragon in your thoughts, hands, and heart and freely fly with him. As you travel with him, the world will become anew with ancient lore for you. Today, you must call Athena, for she is there to lead you to the Dragon Council. Go and fly high, my dear dragon girl Anita. I love you."

Anita, with tears of love and enthusiasm rolling down her cheeks, thanked Kannon and sent her thoughts of love and happiness. Anita walked and lit the candles that were with all the Kannons that resided in her home. At each Kannon, as she lit the candles, Anita sent joyful thoughts of gratitude and love to her. Love and happiness intertwined and whirled in, through and around dear Anita. Smiles and a dragon's laughter led Anita to her office to make a phone call.

"Good morning, Dr. Houston (aka Athena), and how are you today," asked Anita. In her enthusiasm, Anita continued, "I have wonderful news, Dr. Houston! I have been with dragons! I have met Aiki Dragon and his friends Yin and Yang! They are absolutely charming and wonderful! I love being with them! They have invited me to their Dragon Council! I must go immediately! Please show me the way now!"

"Anita, you have everything you need within you to go to the Dragon Council," stated Dr. Houston. "The dragon is one of your archetypes. Archetypes are your links to a much larger and viable reality. You are a hybrid many times over. You are a hybrid of both Cuba and the United States. This is why you love both countries and their people. You are a hybrid of woman and man. You were born a woman yet you have lived in a man's world by being the first woman to do what you've done. Were you not one of the first women in your aviation school to successfully graduate? Were you not one of the first women pilots to be hired at the law firm? A law firm filled with men, where some of them believed that women were too emotional to deal with cases where death is involved? Therefore, it would only be true to life that you are a hybrid of a dragon. Think of your desire to fly at such a young age and making the reality of flight come to life. Think of your ease with the water whether you are floating, swimming, or even deep-sea diving. Remember in your deep-sea diving how you found the underwater life so intriguing, peaceful, and beautiful? You become one with the ocean. Dragons live in the water and fly through the skies. This is why you have no fear of water or flying. Based upon the date of your birth, you are not only a dragon but a water dragon. You are a lucky dragon, for you are both human and dragon! What we need to do now is get you to the Dragon Council! Listen very carefully to my instructions and you will be there safe and sound before you know it. Which is good because the Council and others are waiting for your arrival!"

Anita listened with great intensity and took detailed notes so she could take herself to the Dragon Council. After ending her call with Dr. Houston, Anita wanted to make sure she was dressed properly to be at the Dragon Council. In honor of Kannon, Anita decided to wear all white with gold sandals. In honor of the dragons, Anita wore her gold dragon jewelry. In honor of being invited to the Dragon Council, dear Anita smiled radiantly with all the love and gratitude that was flowing through her heart, body, mind, and soul. My dear Anita was now ready for her journey.

Dear Anita sat comfortably in her chair and closed her eyes. She allowed her mind to totally relax. In her third eye, she placed herself in her spiritual room's closet where in the back was a hidden magical door. Slowly she opened the door and walked through. A grand, winding staircase made of stones was before her. As she stepped down the spiraling staircase, the room was becoming dark and she could hear faint splashing coming from below. Once at the end of the staircase, she found a small wooden raft with a stick attached floating stationary in a wavy river. She stepped on the wooden raft, and vigorously it took her down the narrow river in the dark toward the unknown. In the far distance, she could see a thin beacon of light shining. She began to row toward the light. As she got closer her domain began to fill with the sun's light. She could see that she was nearing a green meadow with a hill. Once at land she docked the boat and ran across the green meadow toward the hill. She ran, ran, ran to reach the top of the hill. At the top of the hill, a tube of light came down from the sky and dear Anita stepped into it. Suddenly, Anita was encased in all bright white light and was zoomed into the sky and on to the Evolutionary University, where all the knowledge of the universe is housed. As she was marveling at all the knowledge within her grasp, she was simultaneously whisked forward to the Dragon Council.

"We welcome you, Anita, with happiness, health, and love to our Dragon Council. We are so pleased to have you in our presence." To dear Anita, these words were heard as if all the Council was saying this to her at the same time. Their thoughts and her thoughts were one. Energies of love and compassion surrounded them all. The Dragon Council was being held on a majestic mountain of rocks of beautiful red monolith. Nature's natural erosion of the monolith allowed for perfect placement and seating for everyone present. The Council consisted of nine powerful and self-assured dragons. The dragons sat similar to the way the nine live oaks surround Anita's home in protection. Anita instinctually, by the feeling of her hara, knew that she was in a safe haven surrounded in the dragons' protection.

My dear Anita looked at the dragons one by one. They were all beautiful to her. Like humans, they all came in different shapes, sizes, and colors. They were the colors of the rainbow! Each had large, artistic eyes of either brown, blue, or green. Except for me, Aiki Dragon. My eyes are of a deep violet that will change to a glowing turquoise when the moon shines upon them. Lucky me! My dear Anita also saw that we dragons have hands with five digits (a thumb and four fingers). Some dragons have only four digits, but we on the Council are of royal blood and are blessed with five. Although we are of royal blood, we never confuse aristocracy with arrogance. Our royalty comes from being of service to others and not being served by others. We love all! All is love! All there is love!

"My dear Anita," I began, "the Dragon Council has asked me to represent them in the matters to be presented to you this morning."

My dear Anita, always kind and gracious, responded, "Yes, Aiki Dragon, tell me everything you wish me to know. My only wish, at this time, is to be of service to you and the Council." When she said her words to me, I could see so much dragon in her. Her face had the invaluable demeanor that we dragons hold dear to us. Upon her face, she carried a smile that was fierce with kindness. Not a fierce that is vicious, but one that is strong with compassion and confidence. Simply breathtaking!

"My dear Anita, we dragons are not of the mythical belief of being mean, fire-breathing, and out to cause destruction to people and their lands. It saddens us to think that humans believe we behave in such a manner. It saddens us, too, to read books or see pictures that depict humans slaying us needlessly and then walking away with false victory for having destroyed us. We dragons are of a benevolent nature. Through our spirituality, we have healing hands that empower mankind. We are fun-loving and filled with laughter and compassion. And we are very wise, as well, for we have lived for thousands and thousands of years. Much longer than mankind. With our wisdom, we know that we must continue to learn and gain more knowledge in all that surrounds our world. Change is always constant even in a dragon's world. We continuously explore in search of new truths that are created and sent out by the spheres of the universe. Although these truths may be new to us, in essence, they are from the beginning of which there is no end. With such truths, we find an abundance of love and kindness that is to be shared with all. Think of dragons as your kindhearted grandparents." It was at this moment that Abuela Ana appeared on the mountain and sat next to dear Anita. In taking her hand she affectionately whispered to Anita, "Listen to Aiki Dragon's words, my dear, for within his heart flows love and wisdom for you and all mankind." Anita gently squeezed Abuela Ana's hand in love and agreement.

"My dear Anita, we dragons want to bring paradise back to Earth. With you being a hybrid, this is possible. As a hybrid, you have a higher frequency of energy that will allow you to go to different dimensions of time, space, realms, and realities. With the consciousness of a hybrid, you will be able to comprehend all that needs to be understood. As a water dragon, you have fluidity and flexibility, allowing you to get everything moving and flowing towards a healing energy. You have healing hands of a dragon in which you can bring dragon energies to the consciousness of mankind. Not only are the energies of Dragon within you, but so are the feelings and emotions of love and laughter. It is through love and laughter that we will create the movements needed to do the most healing of mankind. Think too, of Aikido, my dear

Anita. Of this, we will speak more about in a future Dragon Council meeting. Soon, my dear Anita, I will make an announcement to you that will bring you great pleasure and happiness. The Dragon Councils' hearts smile with love and honor with news within this announcement. For now, though, let's relax and enjoy this beautiful day."

It was a most beautiful day on the mountain for Anita. She went forward to the members of the Dragon Council and gave them warmhearted hugs and words of love and gratitude. They, in turn, hugged and kissed Anita kindly on the cheek. The day's business was done and now it was time to relax and enjoy the beauty of the day. Anita soon discovered that the dragons's belief was the same as hers in the respect of work and play. When you work, you work and no play. When you play, you play and no work. You commit one hundred percent to what you are doing when you are doing it! The Dragon Council mentioned to Anita that they understood her favorite dance to be the cha-cha-cha, to which she eagerly replied, "Yes!"

"Teach it to us," they all cried out.

Within minutes, dear Anita had them dancing! Suddenly, she saw Yin and Yang appear. "Come, you two, let's dance," prompted Anita. Soon the three of them were doing the cha-cha-cha and laughing with all the other dancing dragons. Abuela Ana was laughing and cheering them on!

Soon the Dragon Council indicated that they had to leave due to important business that lay below the ocean's waters. Before leaving they hugged and kissed Anita and showered her with love. "Anita, though we have to go, please stay and enjoy yourself and spend time with Aiki Dragon, Yin and Yang, and your dear Abuela Ana. You are very precious to us, dear Anita, and we look forward to meeting with you again very soon. At that time we will talk more about the universe, the waters, and Aikido. All the blessing of love and beauty to you, dear Anita." Then within a single blink of an eye, they were flying up into the sky, illuminated by the sun's golden rays. Anita watched the splendor of their long dragon forms rise and magnificent dragon wings stretch up and down as they flew. Just for Anita, they flew above her for a few moments in a loving spiral form. Around and around in a loving upward spiral, they flew. Anita knew they were bestowing her an honor in their movements. The dragons' flight into the sky made Anita feel lovingly grounded to the earth, the universe, and the Dragon Realm. Also, she knew, with their spiral movements they were giving her the gift of seeing the power of Aikido in action with the universe. Every cell in Anita's body stood at attention in respect for the love and gift the dragons had shown her. She returned the love and gift by making one powerful thought to be heard by the dragons as they ascended higher—*I am me. I am Dragon. I am you. In love and kindness, I commit to being of service to you forever.*

As the Dragon Council soared higher, Anita could hear the laughter of Yin and Yang. She turned and saw that their cha-cha-cha dancing had turned into feats of acrobats. They were spinning in the air and flying fast through the sky. They were landing on each other's shoulders and tossing each other up high in the air, allowing them to do backward somersaults and land softly on the ground. Then Yin and Yang would take off running and turn cartwheels across the mountain. Anita was in amazement at the speed and accuracy in which they played acrobatic games. They were marvelous! Anita also saw Abuela Ana and Aiki Dragon seated next to each other smiling, talking, and laughing. As she walked toward them, she could see for miles all around her. Behind and below the mountain was the endearing and friendly Lake Titicaca. Above, the sky was a beautiful silky blue with soft, lively white clouds and a pleasantly shining sun.

"My dear Anita, how wonderful it is to spend the day with you and your Abuela Ana," I said. "She and I were just talking about how very proud we are of you in your accomplishments and your ever-growing compassion towards others. You are an angel of love and protection for so many who come into your life, as well as those individuals and spirits that you have empowered unbeknownst to them."

"When you are present love is everywhere," said Abuela Ana.

"I love you, Abuela Ana and Aiki Dragon, so very much," replied Anita with tears of happiness and joy as she sat down between them.

"My dear Anita, I know your tears are of happiness, so let us use that happiness to have smiles and laughter," I said. At my request, for dragons love music, the wind began to play Frederic Chopin's triumphant Waltz Opus 18 from Les Sylphides. This piece is one of our favorites because within it we dragons can feel the elevation of flight, inner strength, playfulness, compassions of a warrior, and love's empowerment within the universe.

"Yin and Yang, please come join us and we shall play a fun game. Everybody, please lie back and look into the sky," I continued (as well as the music of Chopin). Suddenly, the ground beneath us was covered in fine, thick blankets of blues, purples, and pinks, and under our heads were soft pillows. "Now, look into the clouds and let's tell each other what we see," I playfully suggested.

Yin in excitement shouted, "I see a seahorse! I think she must be swimming the deep ocean of blue!"

Yang, sharing in the excitement, resounded, "Yes, we must be looking at the same cloud, for I see a seahorse too! Yet she is floating on the waves of soft blue waters!" Yin and Yang, too excited to remain still, flew up to the seahorse cloud and danced around her in merriment!

I stated, "You know what I see in the clouds? I see a puppy wagging his tail. He is so happy. Like us dragons, he is very happy and loyal to the universe." My dear Anita smiled at me with her beautiful eyes!

Abuela Ana reminisced, "In that cloud, there to the far left, I see my little quincalla. Can you see it too, Anita? Remember you would go there with me in the mornings during the summers when you visited Cuba. We would discuss the different herbs and healing items and the health benefits they produced for those who were in need of remedies. You were always so attentive and inquisitive. You still hold all this knowledge within you. And then after we talked, you would run, faster than the speed of light, to the ocean to swim. Those were such lovely days!"

"My dear Anita, what do you see in the clouds," I asked.

Anita, in sync with her cloud, replied, "I see the silhouette of my father. And now with the movement of the cloud, he is turning his head to face me. I see his loving smile and beautiful sparkling eyes. I can feel his sense of humor. I can feel his love. He is sending me, and all of us, his love. His love is so splendid and powerful. My heart grows happier and happier with his love. How wonderful it is to have him near."

Yin and Yang flew swiftly above and across Aiki Dragon, Abuela Ana, and Anita. "We are going swimming in Lake Titicaca in search of seahorses," they cried in glee.

"What a wonderful idea! Let's all go swimming," I called out.

Abuela Ana stated it was such a beautiful day on land that she wanted to remain on the mountain and enjoy the sun, the music of Chopin, and the clouds. My dear Anita eagerly agreed to go swimming. She quickly shifted her human energies to dragon energies and was flying through the sky with me to Lake Titicaca. We flew around the lake for a while to feel all the positive energy surrounding us. Then we dived headfirst into the waters. Then as quickly as we dove in, we flew out up into the sky. Then back in the waters and out over and over again. No need for a diving board or water slide when you are a dragon! As a dragon, you are your own roller coaster of fun and amusement! Anita and I laughed carefree with excitement. Anita called out for us to go deep into the water and swim. So deep into the water, we dived. Dragons can see perfectly underwater (as they can on land). Once in the water, we saw all types of colorful fish to include the rainbow trout. They swim so harmoniously in their schools. Anita and I were fortunate enough to see the Titicaca water frog. It lives solely underwater. It has a beautiful green skin that is of excess in order to absorb oxygen from the water. As you know frogs are of the water element and symbolize cleansing and healing. They also are like us dragons in that they bring good luck and prosperity. Deeper and deeper we swam in the ocean. As dragons, we can swim underwater indefinitely, like the Titicaca water frog. The deeper we went, the calmer the waters became. Healing powers are found in the waters of Lake Titicaca and all waters throughout the earth. We saw beautiful life-nourishing plants growing in all depths of the lake. We also swam by and admired the pre-Incan mysterious underwater temple that once held fine gold and ceramic figures. What a wonderful time we had swimming and exploring! After swimming, Anita and I floated on the water for a few minutes and admired the beauty of the lake and all the animal life that surrounded it. In the background we could hear Yin and Yang splashing in the water as they played imaginary volleyball!

Then we heard Abuela Ana calling out to dear Anita. We flew quickly to the top of the mountain to Abuela Ana where she was smiling deep in thought. Abuela Ana stated that today had been a magical day for her and that she needed to go, for her husband Pedro was calling her to return home. "Of course, Abuela Ana, it has been a long and magical day for us all. Now it is time for you to have a nice evening with Abuelo Pedro where you can tell him of our day's adventure," lovingly Anita replied.

"I love you, Anita. I am always by your side, in love, and I will see you again soon at the next Dragon Council" said Abuela Ana. Dear Anita hugged Abuela Ana and whispered in her ear how much she loved her and wished her a safe journey home. Then on the softness of the wind's gentle blow, Abuela Ana effortlessly disappeared for home.

"My dear Anita," I said, "it is time for me to leave as well. I want to thank you for this magnificent day of knowledge, fun, and adventure. Your trek here today was one that showed the determination, fierceness, and love of a true dragon. And courage too! You had no fear of the dark staircase or of the dark river that you crossed on a small raft. Please know, my dear Anita, it was the love shining within your heart that created the light you needed to reach the meadow. It also created the light from the sky that ultimately brought you to the Dragon Council. The purity of love's intent will always lead us on a vibrant and brightly shining pathway to where we need to be in our lives. Love's light will always be present with you and lead you to places where beauty and honor forever reside, my dear Anita. So much love. So much light.

"Our next council meeting will be held here very soon. I will come for you prior to the meeting so we may travel together. All my love to you, my dear Anita," I concluded. Then I spread my wings and enclosed them around my dear Anita, embracing her with a tight dragon hug. I could feel the light of her dragon energies warm my wings and heart. Letting go I heard her say, "I love you too, Aiki Dragon." With warmth in my heart, I rose into the sky and flew toward Yin and Yang and let them know it was time to go. The three of us did one quick pass over Anita to show her love and gratitude. She waved, laughed, and applauded us. How wonderful it is to have dear Anita in our World of Dragons!

My dear Anita, enjoying the beauty of all that was around her, decided that she would like to meditate within the depths of Lake Titicaca. Swiftly, on her dragon wings, she flew to the lake and dove deep, deep into its waters. Within her meditation, she began to have indescribable feelings of tranquility and serenity. The pressure of the underwater currents was caressing her gently with feelings of love and kindness. For a few minutes, it was as if no other place existed. There was only the desire to be there within the water and nowhere else. Dear Anita had found a new home. Slowly, dear Anita began to see light coming from the surface of the water to her, and she knew it was me, Aiki Dragon, calling her to return to the land. Instantly, she flew straight out into the sun's warmth and to the top of the mountain. Looking into the sky's clouds, Anita read my message to her—Secrets Are In The Water! Then playfully I shaped a dragon in the clouds to look like Sherlock Holmes holding an oversized magnifying glass. Anita smiled with intrigue and intelligence, for she knew more of the World of Dragons was opening up to her. "Elementary, my dear Aiki Dragon, elementary." Dear Anita chuckled as she took off in flight back to her home.

The next morning, dear Anita woke up with extraordinary feelings of the world's beauty and happiness. She was full of love's energy and ready for the day. After having meditated and said her prayers to Kannon, dear Anita reflected of her previous day at the Dragon Council while drinking a delicious cup of strong Cuban coffee as she sat on her second-floor porch. The sensations of Lake Titicaca's waters still caressed her soft skin with love and happiness. She could hear the birds in the trees singing their beautiful morning songs and could see the squirrels scampering down the trees to gather their morning breakfast of hidden nuts. Iridescent green tree frogs were slowly hopping to the tops of the trees to find sleep after their evening of abounding chirping and frolic. Monarch butterflies and Seepage Dancer dragonflies flew gracefully in the wind. As the wind from the trees blew toward dear Anita, she knew I was once more nudging her with my presence. Gently, I brightened into her view and wished her a good morning. Sweetly she hugged me and bid me a beautiful day. "My dear Anita," I said, "it is a beautiful, sunny, breezy day. The weather is perfect for a new adventure of flying to Dragon Council, don't you agree?"

My dear Anita quickly replied, "Yes! Let's go!" I love my dear Anita's enthusiasm!

"Before we leave, dear Anita, I wanted to tell you a little bit about myself. My soul and spirit are as yours in the respect that they are full of love for all that is around. You are one that is forever wanting to love, teach, help, and protect others because everyone you meet is family in your heart. I, too, am the same. My soul is one that desires to help others as the ancient Indian tribes once did. Remember, I am thousands and thousands of years old. I saw and communicated with those beloved ancient Indian tribes of the Paleo Indians who originally were wanderers throughout North America. They originally came from North Asia (via the Bering Strait) to Alaska (where the polar bears live) and then North America. As life changes and begins anew, so did the Paleo Indians. Their original tribe came to an end, but their spirit was reborn in other Native American tribes and lives on even till today. All these Indian cultures respected each other and the land. They remained as a family unit as they worked, hunted, and planted their land. They were of a strong mind and will. They were survivors and with high esteem and took care of one another, especially their elders. They respected the land and nature. Bison and fish were plentiful back then and nothing went to waste. The Indians used the bison for meat, shelter, and clothes. Fish was food and used as fertilizer for their fields. They grew healthy plants and vegetables. The original Paleo Indians were the first to develop spears made out of stone. They were of a great simple knowledge. Their qualities of pride, love, and compassion live on today. I feel them in my heart and have great respect for them, and this is why I hold them in my soul. This is why I and the other dragons long for mankind to return to paradise and have a healthy and happy existence. We have stayed near mankind all these thousands of years so we may help them. With you, our dream will become a reality, my dear Anita! Take my hand, dear Anita, and let's fly together to the Dragon Council so we may make dreams come to life."

Anita softly reached out and took my hand and together we flew swiftly, like a little girl's red tricycle in pursuit of the heavens, through the air, to the Dragon Council.

On the mountain of the Dragon Council, we landed! What a wonderful feeling it gave my dear Anita to see the Dragon Council once more. The Dragon Council was full of joy, laughter, and humor. So much laughter, for Yin and Yang had been telling them jokes. In honor of Anita, they had one joke especially for her. Yin asked, "Dear Anita, do you know what a cha-cha-cha dancer's favorite food is?"

Anita, already laughing, replied, "No."

Yang quickly answered, "Cha-cha-cha-chorizo with salsa!"

Dear Anita rolled her eyes and laughed even louder! "You two are crazy. A very good crazy, but nonetheless crazy," she kidded. Yin and Yang laughed in good humor with her!

"Welcome once more to our Dragon Council, dear Anita. From our hearts we tell you that it is truly wonderful to see you again," stated the Dragon Council in perfect unison!

"I am so happy and honored to be here with all of you. Please tell me how I may help you. Please tell me what I can do for you," dear Anita replied wholeheartedly.

"You must bring us to light. You must make us visible again. As was mentioned in the last Dragon Council gathering, you have healing hands of a dragon in which you can bring dragon energies to the consciousness of mankind, dear Anita. You must use your healing hands and heart of love and laughter to bring the movement of healing to mankind and the Earth," stated the Dragon Council. As the Dragon Council spoke, Anita could feel a soothing yellow color coming from the other side of the sun to embrace her. Dear Anita knew her Abuela Ana was with her. Love graciously filled her heart and all around her. Anita could also feel the expansion of timelessness. With a gentle push from her Abuela Ana's love, Anita's dragon spirit took her on a flight to the end of the universe, where she could see lines of energy dancing in circular and spiral forms. She could hear the powerful vibration humming sounds the energies created. The past, present, and future presented themselves to Anita as one. Abuela Ana's arm circled around Anita's shoulder as it softly laid its weight upon her. Instantly, Anita was back on the mountain. Abuela Ana whispered knowingly, "Simply beautiful isn't it, my dear?" Dear Anita answered Abuela Ana with a smile and love in her eyes.

I leaned into dear Anita and said, "Your trip was planned in advance by the Dragon Council. They felt this was the best way to show you the truth of feeling meant in the words 'trust in the universe.' In your trip did you not feel courage? It was dragon courage. Do you not feel that timeless information, knowledge, wisdom and infinite love were found in the energies of the universe? All that one needs is found there and given to them through their trust in the universe. No doubt nor fear needs to exist. Only trust. Trust in the universe."

The Dragon Council smiled proudly at dear Anita, for they knew she was learning that which needed to be learned. "Dear Anita, now that you have seen the universe, we want to talk to you about the secrets found in the water. As you know, the earth and the human body each have approximately the same percentage of water, which is around 70 percent. The same is true of dragons. We are 70 percent water. The cells of our bodies, like those of humans, are made up of water. The water in our bodies is representative of our energy. When one is depressed or frightened they tend to remain motionless and blocked. Whereas, someone like yourself, who is filled with love, happiness, and enthusiasm, is full of motion, thus full of energy. One needs to 'shake the water,' so to speak, in order to heal. Does a stream that has been dammed not become overfilled with fallen leaves and mold-covered rocks? That's because the water has slow to no motion. It has low to no energy. Sounds very familiar to your knowledge of Chinese medicine, yes? We dragons, and you, have extraordinary fluidity and flexibility. Our energy levels are naturally high and working at full power at all times on different dimensions. Our high energy allows us to be shapeshifters. You experienced this today in your universal travel. The cells of your body made you the shape, a form of energy, which you needed to be in order to travel out to the end of the universe. With quantum speed, you went from Anita the human to Anita the dragon to Anita the universe. You were one of the dancing spiral energies that you saw. At the same time, you experienced the timelessness of past, present, and future. You are human, dragon, universe, past, present, and future. You are all this at the same time. You are timeless and eternal. Everything and everybody in the universe is as such. Not everybody has this knowledge, though. This is where your healing hands, healing heart, and healing frequency of knowing the secrets of the water come into action. The best way for you to do this is through the movements of Aikido. Aikido is a great vehicle not only for fine-tuning the body, mind, and soul but also for communication, empowerment, and healing through the heart's energy of love. What people need to give them health and happiness is love!"

My dear Anita bowed her head to the Dragon Council in thought and honor of what had just been bestowed upon her. Two tears of compassion and courage rolled from her eyes toward the ground. As the tears rolled from her face, they spiraled around one another and then became one as they landed in the shape of a heart. Love! In the recesses of her thoughts, dear Anita could hear the lines to one of her favorite songs—All you need is love—Love—Love is all you need.

When Anita looked up she could see Kannon (who in the Aikido world is known as Izunome), Su, Confucius, and O'Sensei (the founder of Aikido). All smiled in peace and harmony as they sent her energies of love and thoughts assuring her that she was on the correct path. They were happy and excited for her. In the air, Anita could smell the distinctive manly scent of a familiar cologne. Her father's cologne. She could feel her father's arms surround her in his fatherly embrace. Anita could hear his words kindly say, "We all love you, my dear, and here within your heart and consciousness we all dwell as your protectors and guides as you move forward using your mastery of compassion in the healing art of Aikido. Izunome knows you have a full, balanced heart of love. Su knows you have the instincts of survival that lives within the strengths of a samurai. Confucius knows you have the wisdom and knowledge of a great teacher. Your Abuela Ana knows that you are of true authenticity, which allows for no doubt. O'Sensei gives you the sword of Aiki Guardian, for he knows you are a powerful, compassionate warrior and will be the master of self-victory for yourself and others. And I know you have the integrity, patience, and love needed to be of service in opening up a new world of healing and beauty to mankind."

The Dragon Council silently shook their heads up and down in a yes manner as their passionate dragon energies of courage, joy, laughter, health, and love shined upon dear Anita. "My dear Anita," I began, "I have more exciting news to tell you. You have been a Sensei of Aikido for many years now, and have taught others to defend with love and compassion and for there to be no destructive force within the spiral spheres that you practice. As your new World of the Dragon opens up, you will begin to heal others, and to do as such you must be aware of your uniqueness. You, my dear Anita, are the Dragon Queen Ryu." Dear Anita's eyes opened wider, her heart beat faster with love, and her smile beamed brilliantly as she heard the title being given to her. "As Dragon Queen Ryu you have the two ever-present dragon qualities of fierceness and friendliness within your heart and in your smile," I continued. "You have the wisdom of laughter. Sweet laughter! You are of royal dragon blood and have been blessed with dragon hands and fingers. You have the healing hands and fingers of a royal dragon which you will use in the spiral movements of Aikido to reawaken joyful health and happy souls! Aikido movements mirror the energies of the universe. Think of all the moves in Aikido from the very large to the very small. Remember that the smallest can be the most powerful. In this, I am speaking of the pinky, where great importance and hidden strength can be found. Movements of the hands activate reality. As well as the movements found in the heart and hara."

My dear Anita responded, "Dear Aiki, with all that is me and Dragon, I say to you that I am joyfully overcome with love in all that has been announced to me. My heart dances in rhythm to all the beauties of the universe's energies. My thoughts encompass all of the wisdom that has been enlightened upon me and the knowledge that I am yet to learn. I feel within me the essence of being the Dragon Queen Ryu and all the infinite love that flourishes to be of healing service to mankind. I am eager and ready to use my dragon healing energies!"

"My dear Anita, the gift of healing has always been within you. It has always lived near you and protected you as well. Think of the Hawthorn plant that grows around your home. It is a beautiful healing plant. Its gradual movements of growing upward and spiraling towards the sky allow it to grow stronger. It gains its healing strength through the nourishments in the ground, the rains, and the warmth of the sun's rays. It stores its healing energy until the right time has arrived to heal others. This is you, my dear Anita. You are like the healing gift of the Hawthorn plant. It is now time for you to heal others—mankind. It is not important that they know you are healing them. A Master of Compassion needs no announcement. A Master of Compassion needs not to speak of what needs to be done. A Master of Compassion silently creates that which needs to be created through thought, action, and movement. The mastering of healing is the gift within itself for all. Masa Katsu Agatsu Katsu Hayabi (Self-Victory Is the True Victory Right Now!).

"Do you remember the kindness you showed Bubbles? When he came into your life, he was very ill. Did you turn away from him and not let him in your home? No, instead you took him in your arms, brought him into your home, and gave him the energies of love that allowed him to heal and have a beautiful life. He did not know he was ill. He did not know you were healing him. All he knew was that he was surrounded by love. The energy of love is the strongest energy that will ever exist. Your energies of love manifested into giving him health through compassion, nourishment of body, mind, and soul, positive thoughts of a safe, healthy life, and the movement of body within the protections of your home. As you did all this, your energies were full of love, your voice full of laughter and joy, and your heart full of a dragon's fierce, loving kindness. These will be your Ki (Chi) and guiding forces for healing mankind. Aikido is your universal pasture to healing mankind, my dear Anita. Follow your heart. Follow the feelings found within your hara, my dear Dragon Queen Ryu!"

Chapter 15

Aikido Anita

Masa Katsu Agatsu Katsu Hayabi

Aikido. Ai—Ki—Do. Ai—Ki—Do! Ai—Harmony. Ki—Spirit. Do—the Way. Aikido! My dear Anita had learned of the word Aikido while in law school. She read the book *The Spirit of Aikido,* and its words embraced her heart. Martial arts were nothing new to Anita. She had studied successfully the mental and physical training of karate. She enjoyed the mental concentration and physical movements of karate, but she never felt at one within her heart in the destructiveness of karate's intent to kill your attacker. Too much love lived in my dear Anita to want to do harm to another. Anita wanted her love to protect and benefit another instead. A form of healthy healing for others silently lived in my dear Anita's soul. It lived so silently within dear Anita that even she had not heard its voice. With the introduction to Aikido, though, came the compassionate feelings of healthy healing harmoniously throughout her body, mind, and soul. True compassion that involves the martial arts is not a weakness or a form of passiveness, but rather a commitment of great strength and trust that comes naturally from the heart to help and guide those to find their inner truth whether or not their original intent was to cause harm or good. My dear Anita understood that the fierce, compassionate powers found in the spirituality of Aikido do not discriminate between foe and friend. All are to be treated the same to ensure the equality of enlightenment to their life's well-being. Anita's heart told her that when she had the time to fully dedicate herself, she would begin to physically and spiritually train in the movements that interweave with Aikido's meaning of harmony, spirit, and the way!

As time moved forward in my dear Anita's life, she realized that the Aikido qualities of calmness and confidence were ever present in her daily thoughts and movements. Enthusiasm was pulsating throughout her as she read another Aikido book, *Aikido and the Harmony of Nature*. Within the book's pages, the word "dojo" and its meaning (place of enlightenment) kept lighting up in her thoughts and heart. My dear Anita knew now was the appointed time to dedicate herself to Aikido! Quietly, I cheered her on, whispering to her, "Follow your heart. Follow your feelings from the hara." My dear Anita, in perfect posture, and looking straight and smiling, stepped forward with her hara on the path to her green pasture of Aikido!

My dear Anita was a dedicated student. The studying and training of Aikido are for those of a courageous heart, for it does not happen overnight. It takes years of discipline and commitment. In fact, it takes more than years—it takes a lifetime of devoutness. The first thing dear Anita did was to let go of all ego (of which there was almost none). There is no place for any ego in Aikido. Enthusiasm was her spirit! Her spirit was her energies and thoughts. Her energies and thoughts revealed to her three principles: Trust Yourself. Trust in Your Training. Trust in the Universe.

My dear Anita in her beginnings of Aikido remembered the words that Confucius's wisdom had told her, which were "not to worry, for you will know what to do." Trust! Thus, her three principles of Trust ruled unanimously with compassion, authenticity, and precision. There was no need for and there was no doubt. Abundantly, in my dear Anita's heart-centered consciousness flowed love, courage, joy, laughter, and health for herself and others.

Perseverance prevailed for dear Anita. She had the velocity of a spinning top of perfect alignment to that which surrounded her. And like a spinning top, she gathered all the energy around her. Aikido in Houston was not well-known at the time, and dear Anita wanted to learn all the information she could gather. She did not see this as a deterrent, though. Anita went to more than one Aikido association to learn and train. Doing so reminded her of a tale of good luck vs. bad luck. The tale goes as such:

There was a Chinese farmer and his wife who owned only an old horse that the son used to work the land. One morning the son found the fence broken and the horse gone. Good luck or bad luck? The son found the horse with a herd of young, healthy horses. Good luck or bad luck? When training one of the wild horses, he was thrown and broke his leg. Good luck or bad luck? The emperor declared war and all young men must go to battle. When the soldiers arrived for the son, they did not take him because of his broken leg. Good luck or bad luck?

Dear Anita will tell you that the moral of this tale is that you cannot judge what happens to you. Trust in the universe and that everything that happens is for your own good. In short, the necessity to go to different associations to study and train Aikido did not detour or discourage Anita. To her, this opened up more worlds of Aikido that she could explore and participate in.

My dear Anita has always had the joy of a child within her heart and soul, which has given her an ease of learning. She has always had the excitement and enthusiasm of a little girl when it comes to knowledge. The world to her is like going to the circus! She has her circus brochure of the show's events and reads it from beginning to end and commits to memory all the names of the performers and animals. Dear Anita is now prepared for the show to begin! In her seat, she waits both eagerly and patiently for that which is to be presented to her. Then as the rhythmic drummers march, the spinning clowns roll, and the high trapeze acrobats fly into the arena, dear Anita becomes at one with them in their movements and merriment. This is how she has the ease of learning. Dear Anita prepares and becomes that which she is learning! My dear Anita becomes knowledge in motion!

My dear Anita, as you have learned, is one who commits to her quest to learn, and so along with the various Aikido associations, she began private one-on-one training with Aikido senseis (teachers) and yudanshas (black belt rank holders). At the beginning of dear Anita's Aikido training, it was very important that she remain more focused on the physical than the spiritual elements of the martial arts. Dear Anita's Aikido movements had her and her uke (the opponent being thrown) literally flying through the air. A dragon's energy of flight was in my dear Anita's movements. Though her focus was on the physical elements, Anita's heart whispered kindness and happiness through her eyes to her uke, which allowed both of them to smile in triumph at all times! Smiles and laughter create immeasurable strengths and deter fear. Aikido, as you will be discovering, is freedom from fear!

Aikido movements came naturally to dear Anita, especially in her hands. As a small child, dear Anita, for hours in her crib, would turn her hands in spiral forms, back and forth in the Aikido movement of Kuko. And as she spun her hands, she would sing a sweet little song to herself—"Little dragons open their wings big in the sky. Around the universe, they fly. Wishing love and joy to you and I."

With gratitude and graciousness in her heart, Anita received her first-degree black belt degree four years later (for with her perseverance time went as needed to learn all that she needed to learn)! Although this was a most wonderful attainment, to her it was only the beginning! She had more degrees in black belts to achieve! Now my dear Anita's mind, like her spirit, is always heading forward in thought and movement. She had already found the name Shobu Aikido Houston for her path into Aikido. Dear Anita loved the names Shobu, meaning wisdom, and Aikido, meaning harmony, spirit, and the way. And Houston was home in her heart. With her first movement of Aikido, dear Anita knew that universal ki would be inviting the personal ki of peaceful, compassionate warriors into her expanding world.

It gave me such joy to see my dear Anita filled with happiness and determination as she moved forward into Aikido. It made me think of her as the smiling little girl who set off to fly to the heavens with her tricycle. For she was doing the same now. She was flying high with smiles and laughter in the movements of Aikido! The universe was spinning lovingly around my dear Anita as she reposefully spun in spirals with it.

There is a wondrous place where my dear Anita and I meet to have our own private retreats with our thoughts and to be at one with all that is within the universe. We meet on the top of a small mountain where we feel the warming sun, cooling breeze, and harmony of nature. It is our special playground where we can tell jokes, discuss philosophy, and ask each other for words of wisdom. I used to come here often and enjoy the solitude of its peacefulness before I made myself known to dear Anita. Within the view of this small mountain are nine monumental mountains. I use the word monumental due to its enormous stature and celebratory phenomena. For I and the other dragons of the council, when we are on land, live in these majestic mountains. And since my dear Anita is the Dragon Queen Ryu, she is a part of these mountains as well. Around the tallest of these mountains was set into place my dear Anita's spiral spiritual path of Aikido. Though she does not remember, for it is meant to be as such, she used to visit these mountains regularly in her dreams. I was always there in silence, love, and guidance as she trekked these mountains. These mountains are of her life. It was not accidental that the largest mountain was meant for Aikido. My dear Anita needed plenty of climbing space to learn more, practice, teach, celebrate, and welcome fellow compassionate warriors. Just as spectacular as the mountain is my dear Anita!

My dear Anita began traveling throughout the United States to Aikido seminars. Techniques, techniques, and more techniques breathed continuity within dear Anita's mind and body. In hanmi (the triangular stance of Aikido where all techniques begin) and through her hara (where all movements originate), dear Anita rediscovered her gratefulness for the earth's gravity, for she knew it made her connected to the center of the earth's solidity of metal and iron, allowing her to initiate her spiral movements of the universe's unified motions. Her soul knew there was more for her to learn in regard to Aikido's spirituality, as well, but patiently it waited knowing that the knowledge would be presenting itself in a unique manner in the very near future.

An Aikido seminar in Phoenix, Arizona, touched my dear Anita's heart and soul. The seminar was held in the gymnasium of an old Catholic high school. Walking through the high school brought back memories to dear Anita of the days she was in Catholic elementary school. She remembered all the nuns, the studying, the fun of chasing a little boy for a kiss, and the quest to be a missionary. Her heart was beating passionately with love of the past's teachings and happiness for the future Aikido's learnings. As my dear Anita walked into the gymnasium, her heart's beating of love and happiness stayed with her. She was joyously overcome with a great sense of peace as she waited in the gymnasium for the seminar to begin. Then with no announcement, the teacher of the seminar entered. A sunray of warmth, named Mitsugi Saotome Shihan (a master teacher), shined upon dear Anita. A man of five-foot-two, with impeccable posture, dressed in his handsome clothes (designed and made by him), cowboy boots, and hat, was smiling, talking, and making jokes with the students as he hugged them warmly using the peaceful love from his heart. My dear Anita could feel the peaceful love from his heart enter hers and she knew, without any doubt, that the powers of Aikido's spirituality had just entered her universe.

Each day of the three-day seminar filled dear Anita more and more with boundless Aikido admiration and enthusiasm. The times that Anita practiced with Saotome Sensei was beyond words. It was all in the feelings of the techniques and movements that they shared in practice. Saotome Sensei brought up a seven-foot-four man to the center of the gymnasium to show the students how size does not matter between an uke and a nage (the one who throws). Saotome Sensei, with a smile, looked at the man from the bottom of his feet to the top of his head. Then he requested they both stand side by side to show the students the vast difference between their sizes. Then both faced one another in hanmi. And with the slightest movement, as if to sneeze, the tiny Sensei had the huge man flying up and down to the ground. The kindest of smiles and laughter filled the man, Saotome Sensei, and the students. Saotome Sensei said to the class, "You must have sharpness and compassion. No ego. No intent to hurt or harm. This now why we have laughter and smiles." My dear Anita and the room were filled with Saotome Sensei's peaceful love!

This peaceful love let dear Anita instantaneously know that she wanted to be a part of Saotome Sensei's founded Aikido school. At the end of the seminar she went before him and stated, "Sensei, I would like to become part of the Aikido Schools of Ueshiba. I want to be of your organization."

Saotome Sensei looked sharply into her face and yelled (not in meanness, but in endearment for all), "No organization. This family. You read *Aikido Today Magazine*. I write story. You then understand why this family." Saotome Sensei warm-heartedly smiled and hugged dear Anita and then turned and left without saying another word. Unfortunately for Anita, she did not have a chance to say another word either, but she felt Sensei's peaceful love still within the room and her heart. The Aikido Schools of Ueshiba were still in her heart as well.

The following morning after dear Anita got back home to Houston, she called the Aikido Schools of Ueshiba and was connected to a man who told her that to be considered as a member of the school, she would need a sponsor. Anita explained that there was no one in Houston who could sponsor her. He asked her to hold the line. The next voice she heard was that of a woman. Dear Anita, in her direct and compassionate Attorney Anita tone, explained to the woman her reasons why she was determined to become a part of the school and that she could not get a local sponsor. The woman on the other end simply said, "I'll sponsor you." The woman was Patty Saotome. Saotome Sensei's wife. Synchrodestiny again in motion.

My dear Anita told me once that Aikido is like dancing in the respect that you need two to dance. So true. Dear Anita needed Aikido partners in order to practice. There was a school that she attended where she could train and also teach. She enjoyed teaching the students. Her class grew larger and larger, which to her was wonderful. The more students to practice with filled her heart with joy. The more students the more everyone benefited in their training. Everyone got to learn from everyone. Sometimes, though, as Abuela Ana had once explained to dear Anita, other's fear can attempt to enter your world. The school where Anita taught was run by a father and daughter team. Anita's growing class was due to the enthusiasm that she put into the practice. She and her students created the peaceful ki needed for the art of Aikido. Students were coming from the other classes that the school held. Most specifically, many of the students were leaving the daughter's classes to participate in Anita's. The daughter did not like this fact, because it made her fearful that Anita may start her own school and take the students away. Without warning, Anita's class was abruptly canceled.

Now at first, you may think this was bad luck for Anita. But it truly was good luck. You see, Abuela Ana, from the heavens, was aware of what was happening and was not going to allow anything to happen to dear Anita. Abuela Ana surrounded dear Anita with more love. She also surrounded the daughter's image in a jar filled with honey to keep dear Anita from being touched by any malice or fear. Abuela Ana did a beautiful job! Abuela Ana's love was victorious for dear Anita! It was due to Abuela Ana's protection of Anita that the class was canceled. The act of discontinuing Anita's class created a new path of Aikido for her. My dear Anita decided that she would build a dojo of her own to practice and teach students Aikido! The daughter's fear created what she did not want to happen—for Anita to build her own school. Anita being honorable did build her own school, but did not take any of the daughter's students away. Abuela Ana's love was victorious for dear Anita!

My dear Anita's home, at the time, was built on four acres of land that was near a bayou. On the land, there were beautiful tall trees that reached high into the sky. Due to the bayou and splendor of the trees, dear Anita had a treehouse dojo built within the trees. The dojo was twenty-six feet in the sky, and a spectacular, curving, almost spiraling red bridge led the way from the earth to the heavens where its front door awaited to welcome all who entered. Of course, this dojo did not happen overnight. Much thought and planning went into the design. As a matter of fact, dear Anita had two rocket scientist friends from NASA to share the sketch of their dojo's mat to help her design the aerodynamics, if you will, of its co-existence to sway safely in harmony with the blowing wind within the nestling trees.

The time it took to have the dojo completed was a blessing for dear Anita. She used this time wisely to design the shomen for O'Sensei (the great teacher of Aikido). O'Sensei was born in Japan in 1883 and given the birth name of Morihei Ueshiba. O'Sensei from an early age was an avid reader with great interests in religion, poetry, and art. As a boy, he saw his father being attacked and realized the need for strength and self-defense. O'Sensei's great-grandfather had been a great samurai. As a young man, O'Sensei studied several martial arts (including Jujutsu) and various religions (including Shinto and Buddhism primarily due to his mother's strong spirituality). O'Sensei was a soldier in the Japanese army during the Russo-Japanese War. O'Sensei was a strong-willed individual. Originally, he was denied into the army due to being shorter than the five-foot-two requirement. He tied weights to his legs and hung and swung in the trees to lengthen his legs. O'Sensei always kept spirituality close to his heart and thoughts: therefore, they made a profound impact on his views of the martial arts. He founded his own style of martial arts, Aikido, which introduced the spiritual concepts of love, compassion, and peace. A compassionate warrior does not kill or destroy their opponent, but rather uses the power of love to prevent harm. With his passing in 1969, O'Sensei's deshis (students), of which Saotome Sensei is one, were left with the honor of keeping the Aikido tradition.

In her design of the shomen, dear Anita included a photo of O'Sensei, shelves to present him flowers, and a large ceiling-to-floor Japanese calligraphy that read Ai Ki Do! The spirit of Aikido was present in the shomen and throughout the dojo. Dear Anita also had placed the beautiful figurine of Kannon (Izunome) that Mr. Tanaka had given her, on her desk facing the dojo doors so all entering may be blessed by her. Also, dear Anita knew that O'Sensei loved Izunome and held her spiritually within his heart and body. It gave my dear Anita great joy and happiness to know that she was expressing love and honor to both O'Sensei and Izunome within the sanctuary of her dojo.

Once the dojo was opened there was no fanfare. No big celebration. Instead, there was a dedication of spirit, body, and mind to the techniques and truths of Aikido! There was daily training of courage and compassion. There was also breakfast! The classes in the dojo were morning classes starting at 8:00 sharp; therefore, breakfast must follow for all those hungry warriors! My dear Anita insisted that everyone have a hearty breakfast! After Aikido classes the deshis would leave the dojo and return to Anita's home. They would walk in the air, using the red winding bridge, from the tops of the trees to the soil of the ground that led to the first level of dear Anita's home. As they walked they could see the magnificent grounds come closer toward them. Within this terrain of four acres, great nature lived. Dear Anita's yard was like a little forest with lots of tall, towering trees and large, prolific plants. Beauty and harmony were everywhere. The bayou's flowing waters would gently hum the spirit of tranquility. Squirrels ran playfully chasing each other from tree to tree! The blue jays, cardinals, robins, herons, and tiny sparrows sang sweet melodies throughout the day. The colorful dragonflies and butterflies would dance in delight as they fluttered around the blooming plants. Hummingbirds would join in their dance as they drank nectar from the blooms. Nine growing koi fish swam by, flexing their bodies and tails in vigor as the cool waters of a waterfall fell soothingly upon them. Possums, raccoons, and coyotes would unite as they visited in the early evenings. Late at night, a grandfatherly owl would hoot while keeping company with sweet Bubbles as he played in the moon's beams.

And breakfast was just as magnificent as the little forest! Upon entering the first level of the house, which was dear Anita's gym, a wonderful spread of food would be waiting for them. Scrambled eggs, pancakes with maple syrup, bagels with cream cheese and salmon, and fresh fruits of berries, melon, and bananas! Lots of freshly squeezed juice and hot tea!

The conversations over breakfast would be held around a much-loved table of Anita's (it was one of the many treasures given to her by Mr. Tanaka). The discussions would be of great topics to include world events, each other's lives, and the mutual fascination all had for Aikido. Breakfast was always nourishing both physically and mentally! What a wonderful way to start the morning—Aikido, breakfast, and laughter with friends! The same was true for the children's classes dear Anita held on Saturday mornings. After breakfast, the children did not want to leave. The young warriors would stay until late afternoon so they could play in the little forest using their Aikido imaginations to explore flourishing new worlds filled with the harmony of love and compassion!

Let me explain to you why the students were always ready for breakfast! Dear Anita started the class off with 500 repetitions of abdominal exercises, which were done within five minutes. If you were a sleepyhead at 8:00 a.m., these exercises would wake all your body up in a hurry! Have you ever done 500 abs in five minutes? It is a feat not for the faint of heart! One should always be proud of completing 500 abs in five minutes. Of course, this was just icing on the cake, if you will, for dear Anita. In her personal daily exercise routine, she incorporated additional abdominal exercises. Anita jokingly told me once that she had to remain the same size as she was when she was sixteen because of the gold chain she started wearing around her waist at that age. She concluded that gold had become too expensive to have a larger size made! My dear Anita is both humorous and practical at the same time!

Anita's deshis were from the beginning kyu (white belt) through the experienced yudanshas. The main emphasis in the dojo, in the beginning, was on Waza (technique). Learning the movements. Dedication, practice, and compassion were the triumphant energies created between dear Anita and the students. Are you familiar with the motto of the Three Musketeers—One for all and all for one? This was the camaraderie found within my dear Anita's dojo. The method of teaching and learning became one. For as you learn you teach, do you not? You teach yourself that which needs to be learned. You also share your knowledge of competence with your teacher. Through you, your teacher is able to learn. What a wonderful gift this is to your teacher.

In Aikido the deshis are before each other in pairs, thus the uke and nage teach and learn simultaneously. Whether they are standing in hanmi or seated in seiza, all are in kamae (the stance of readiness). The uke and nage's beginning spiral movements are the mirrored images of one another. They cannot read the other's thoughts, but they see and feel each other's movements and energies as they spin toward each other. At this moment, the uke and nage's energies are beginning to intertwine into the other's sphere. Musubi (the modus operandi of the ki's unification) has been created! As the deshis continue their spiral movements and enter their techniques, the nage connects to the uke's energy and uses it to have a peaceful and compassionate resolution. There is no winning or losing between the uke and nage. There is no force or competitiveness. There is only the noncompetitive act of peace to not allow others to harm you or you to do harm to others. You see, in Aikido although the knowledge and skill to kill or destroy is known, the harmonious, compassionate warrior chooses to do otherwise. Takemusu Aiki (Enlightened Aikido)!

There is an ancient tale about the wind and the sun that may help to explain in a different light the power of peace and compassion in dealing with opposing forces. One day the Wind was bragging to all that were near him about how powerful and great he was. He claimed that with force like his, everything and everybody was under the will of his commands. The Sun had been listening to all the Wind had to say and she noticed that the rivers were slowing down, the little animals of the forest were hiding, blooms were closing, and the birds were flying away. The Sun was thinking to herself what a bully the Wind had become and that he was behaving without chivalry or kindness and he was causing the balanced beings of the universe to withdraw and become out of harmony. *Enough is enough,* the sun said to herself, for she could not bear to see the beings suffering. "Mr. Wind," the Sun radiantly called out, "the day is beautiful and I don't believe there is any need for you to be so blustering to all that is around us."

The Wind replied, "Listen, Ms. Sun, I am stronger than you and I'll do as I please. Besides, these rivers, plants, and animals are nothing without me. I am the most powerful of all!"

We shall see, the Sun thought loud enough to herself so all the beings could feel her loving energy. "Mr. Wind," the Sun said with a gentle smile, "I have more power in one single ray of light than you have in all your gusts." The Sun was not being boastful, for that was not of her nature. She was being noble in her forewarning to the Wind, for she knew within her heart that the power of peace and love had the capability to overcome acts of discord or ego.

The Wind immediately blew the clouds to cover the Sun and stated, "No, I am most powerful. Let's compete. The next Villager that comes by, we will have them remove their coat." The Sun agreed. In her wisdom, she remained behind the clouds, allowing the day to be darker and cooler. Soon a Villager was walking in haste and distress on the chilly, darkened path in the forest. The Wind blew strong cold winds toward the Villager to force their coat off. The Villager only held on tight to their coat. The Wind blew colder winds and rain clouds upon the Villager, soaking them. The Villager tightened their coat even tighter. Eventually, the Wind died down. With the slightest of movement the Sun shined bright and evaporated the clouds away. As she shined, the day became brighter and warmer. She continued to shine her warmth upon the Villager. The Villager removed their coat and took in the Sun's loving warmth and light as they began to walk in peace with a large smile and laughter. And all the beings that were within the forest felt her warmth and love, as well, and became at one with her. The rivers flowed stronger. The little animals came out of hiding and ran freely to and fro. The blooms opened larger and fuller of color. And the birds returned to the trees and began building their nests.

The Sun, unlike the Wind, used no force. She used the techniques of peace and compassion found naturally inside of her. Harm to the Wind or Villager was never in her thoughts. Nor was there any competition. The Sun did not win or lose. She was though victorious! Victorious because without ego she taught the Wind a valuable lesson. The Sun enlightened the Wind to the true strength of power. Outside brawn and force do not make for power. Inner peace and love create a compassionate energy that creates a harm-free universal power that is beneficial to all in the universe. Think about it. The Sun's warmth and love benefited the Wind, the Villager, and all the beings (and future beings) in the forest. They all became wiser, stronger, and happier. This is a lesson of Aikido.

The beginning of the dojo proved to be a very busy time for my dear Anita. She was giving morning classes (and serving breakfast!) three days a week. Dear Anita was traveling throughout the United States to attend Aikido seminars and workshops. She was continuing to read all the books and magazines she could find regarding Aikido. Dear Anita was writing journals of all she was learning. Plus, she was creating a teaching manual that would hold all the training plans for each class. During this time, dear Anita decided to give up her career as an attorney. No more law (neither full time nor part time). Aikido was her definitive path. Aikido was her infinite passion. Anita's father, Mr. Arango, had jokingly said to her, "You're giving up a successful law career so you can kick people?" Mr. Arango was a wise man and he knew there was much more to Aikido than kicking people! He saw how Anita's face lit up and heard how her voice filled with enthusiasm when she discussed Aikido with him. Radiating from her he could see the wisdom of Aikido's philosophy of peace and harmony being renewed and coming to full life through her confident and compassionate spirit. It was just like the days when she was a rambunctious little girl and the two of them would talk for hours of Confucius. He knew that

Anita cherished and lived with Confucius's words. Mr. Arango's heart was filled with happiness knowing his sweet, rambunctious little girl's evolving path of life was enriched with an abundance of universal truths, wise words, harmonious strengths, and love's compassion. He knew, too, that Aikido was the harmony, energy, and way that Anita was to become forever one with!

My dear Anita's sponsor, Patty Saotome, began to visit the dojo twice a year. When she came she would bring her own ukes to assist Anita and the deshis in their Aikido training. Dear Anita trained one on one with Patty with her tachi (sword) techniques. It was a pleasure to have Patty Saotome in the dojo. The universal ki and personal ki flowed equally and harmoniously with all! Compassion's determination, laughter, and smiles were ever-present!

During Patty Saotome's first visit to the dojo, she announced that dear Anita had been accepted as a member of the Aikido Schools of Ueshiba. Joy and jubilation filled my dear Anita's heart and flowed over into the dojo and all the deshis! This was a wonderful time for celebration!! Soon dear Anita would be in Phoenix celebrating once again with Patty Saotome, Saotome Sensei and the ASU family. Dear Anita brought a case of red wine to the celebration, which proved to be very popular with the ASU family! In Aikido there is a saying "Expect Nothing and Be Ready for Everything!" My dear Anita's membership to the ASU was one of those moments!

In Aikido there is one word that moves forward like no other. The word is "hara." The hara is located in the lower abdomen approximately two inches below the navel. As dear Anita explained to her deshis, the hara is the center of life's energy. Movement and ki originate from the hara. When training in Aikido one should always stay focused on the hara, for it gives one composure and a relaxed state of mind for any situation that may present itself. The spiritual energy will travel from the hara through the heart, the mind, and the body as it moves forward and is put into action. Just the slightest touch from a nage's finger to an uke can cause them to lose their balance and fall effortlessly to the ground without any harm. Great strength comes from within the hara. Great energies of love, kindness, and compassion come from within the hara.

The hara also has a strength of fearlessness. Courage lives within the hara. The way one stands and moves with their hara tells much about them. Your hara much like involuntary muscles creates movement without thought. Let me tell you a story involving my dear Anita while she lived in New York. It was after lunch and dear Anita was returning to work in the Pan Am building. As she was walking through the parking lot, she noticed a large man was hiding behind a pole. Anita kept walking and entered the building and headed toward the elevator. She did not see the man enter the building. In her stride, she moved forward with her mind not on the man, but on herself. She could feel the strength being generated within her hara. Her stride was one of swiftness, but not overly fast. No need to rush. Her posture was upright and full of confidence. And her head was level and facing forward toward the elevator and her arm automatically, without thought, pushed the elevator call button. The elevator door opened and three people exited, leaving the elevator empty. Dear Anita stepped in the elevator and pushed the 50th-floor button. In pushing the button she looked directly out the elevator to see the man approaching with great speed. The elevator door was closing, almost shut, when the man put his elbow between the two doors, causing them to open. He hastily stepped into the elevator, blocking the exit by standing in front of the doors. He did not push a button to any floor. As a compassionate warrior, my dear Anita could feel the vibrations of the man's intentions, and they were not of the honorable kind. Anita greeted him all-knowingly with a smile and direct eye contact as she calmly stated, "It's a very nice day." The man was taken aback. He did not expect this from a petite five-foot-two woman. A few moments later as the elevator door began to open on the 50th floor, the man heartlessly fled. Dear Anita, as if nothing had happened, got off and went to her office to continue the day's work.

My dear Anita knew though that something had happened. It remained in her thoughts. She was aware of the strength of her hara and how it intuitively opened her up to dealing with fear. Fear is not always a bad thing. Fear does not always mean one must frightened, but rather to be aware of danger and face the situation in a calm manner. Dear Anita's hara led her fearlessly into a center of calm with the man (her opponent). The energies from her hara did not make him a wrong or evil person, but simply one whose bad intentions needed to be quickly defused without harm. Her hara effortlessly manifested her to safety by presenting fearlessness, compassions of love and no ill will, and a connection of both Anita's and the man's energies. Anita turning, making eye contact, and speaking to the man caused him trepidation. The courage exuded from dear Anita's hara gave him fear. It was not Anita's fear, but that of his own. In short, he became powerlessly fearful of her and lost his state of mind, confidence, and courage. This is another lesson of Aikido!

As training and practicing Aikido progressed in the dojo, so did the degrees of black belts for my dear Anita. Shortly after receiving her fourth black belt degree, she attended one of Saotome Sensei's seminars where another moment of "Expect Nothing and Be Ready for Everything" occurred. Dear Anita arrived late to the seminar due to the delay of her plane taking off. Once she arrived at the seminar, Saotome Sensei was already in the front of the dojo (where he designed the shomen) explaining the technique of Irimi Nage. Dear Anita quietly entered the dojo and silently waited for Saotome Sensei's acknowledgment for her to enter onto the practice area of the dojo. Usually, a Sensei will speak a simple word or a hand wave directing the deshi to enter. Saotome Sensei saw my dear Anita and left the mat to welcome her into the seminar and practices with a hug. He began asking her how she had been and how very happy he was to see her. He also asked her, "Why you no Juku?" As dear Anita was beginning to answer, Saotome Sensei looked to the representatives of the ASU and stated, "She need Juku!" My dear Anita said to Saotome Sensei that she presently held no higher than a fourth-degree black belt. "No matter. No testing. Juku independent rank or status. You Juku today," proclaimed Saotome Sensei. The induction of a Juku is not an everyday event given casually to a deshi. An honor of honors had been awarded to Anita. She had just received the honorable title of Ueshiba Juku. Such an honor may only be given by a true Uchi Deshi of O'Sensei, and Saotome Sensei was one of only a few. To be an Ueshiba Juku declares the individual is a direct disciple of Saotome Sensei and an inheritor of his teachings. It also recognizes them as being a part of O'Sensei's school and pure lineage. To commemorate the honor, dear Anita was given a formal dogi (Aikido uniform) with a hand-embroidered special kanji that only those given such an honor may wear.

Dear Anita and Saomote Sensei were very much alike in the respects of their lives and hearts, which spiritually bonded them. Saomote Sensei as a young man studied in judo and to be an engineer. At age seventeen, with the referral of his judo master, he was presented to O'Sensei at his school of Aikiai Hombu Dojo. At their first meeting, O'Sensei called Saotome Sensei to join him to talk privately. Spiritually there was an immediate bond between them, and shortly thereafter Saotome Sensei became his Uchi Deshi. Saotome Sensei remained constantly by O'Sensei's side until his death in 1969. In 1975, after several days of meditation, he believed it was the wishes of O'Sensei for him to leave Aikiai Hombu Dojo and begin an Aikido school of his own in the United States.

My dear Anita and Saotome Sensei's spiritual bond was immediate very much the same way when dear Anita first met him at the seminar in the old Catholic school gymnasium. There was an instant rapport between the two. Just as O'Sensei had given Saotome Sensei the spiritual calling of Aikido, so had Saotome Sensei given to dear Anita. Just like the way Saotome Sensei ended his studies to be an engineer, dear Anita ended her career as an attorney. She knew that Aikido was what her future held. At the next seminars, dear Anita told Saotome Sensei, in happiness and gratitude, that his compassion of peace and love was the reason behind her giving up her career and dedicating herself to Aikido. The beauty and pure honesty in dear Anita's words gave Saotome Sensei tears of joy. He quickly left with only giving dear Anita a hug. No more words were necessary, though, for the spirit of Aikido they shared had compassionately spoken to each other's heart all that needed to be said. Dear Anita felt Saotome Sensei's energies of a wise, compassionate warrior flow gently into her heart and spiral throughout her body and mind.

Love, happiness, beauty, and new awareness shined brightly from my dear Anita's spirit. Saotome Sensei through his love and the guidance by O'Sensei's spirit had just spiritually given dear Anita the beautiful gift of misogi. Saotome Sensei's hug and tears of joy released the purification of mind, body, and spirit for dear Anita. Purification in the respect that it enlightened her spiritual keiko (study) of Aikido. Misogi had awakened dear Anita's Dragon Queen Ryu. Gradually, yet powerfully more changes and awareness would be presenting themselves on dear Anita's path of compassion and courage. Love, happiness, and beauty shined brightly from her spirit as she left the seminar and returned home to her dojo in Houston.

My dear Anita had a beautiful dream three days after returning from Saotome Sensei's seminar. It was of a young and slightly naïve (due to his newness in the world), yet determined baby dragon named Little Irimi Nage. Little Irimi Nage being new to the world was very small and light in weight. He was born on the small mountain where Anita and I would meet. Little Irimi Nage had a baby dragon's quest to meet Anita and tell her how much he loved her. He had never met Anita but had seen her gentleness and kindness as she and I would talk on the mountain. One early morning, he told his mother that he was going to fly into the universe to meet a beautiful dragon queen. His mother thought he was just playing and was going to imagine to travel as he sat in safety on the tree's branches, so she wished him a fun trip and told him to be home for lunch. With a smile and excitement, he opened his wings and flew up into the sunny blue sky with the vision of dear Anita in his heart. A few moments later, the soft breeze became a hard wind that seemed to be fighting with Little Irimi Nage. Although he was not frightened, he began to lose his concentration and struggled with the wind as he flew forward. The wind was taking the breath out of him. He began to feel lost both physically and emotionally. He was beginning to get angry at the wind and himself. In his anger, the wind appeared to get stronger and he weaker. Suddenly, dear Anita's vision came back into his thoughts. A calmness overtook his spirit. All he could feel was love and harmony within himself and of the wind. There was no more struggle. Little Irimi Nage allowed the wind to come to him as he gently grabbed the wind's energy and spun the two of them together using full control of their energies to resolving the wind's intent in a harmless manner. The wind laughed in admiration of Little Irimi Nage's courage, and through the laughter the rain clouds dissipated. Little Irimi Nage felt the strength that his courage had created for him. It was a strength not of ego or of being better, but one of wishing another only protection and no harm. With gratitude, he thanked the wind for teaching him such a wonderful lesson.

As he flew away he was thinking to himself that he could not wait to tell Anita of his adventure. Soon Little Irimi Nage was flying above dear Anita's home, and he saw her walking across the grounds. He was very excited to meet her and say hello. Joyfully and with a baby dragon's exuberance he called out, "Hello, dear Anita, I am Little Irimi Nage and how wonderful it is to see you!" Dear Anita looked up and with a slight laugh of pure love smiled at Little Irimi Nage. "Dear Anita, you don't know me, but I am a friend of yours," he said.

Dear Anita in sweetness replied, "You look very familiar to me, little one; therefore, I must know you and it brings happiness to my heart to be speaking with you." Little Irimi Nage proudly told dear Anita of his adventure with the wind. "What a victorious dragon warrior you are, Little Irimi Nage. You learned a wonderful lesson today of trust in yourself and love of others. Your courage created peace. You will always be victorious, little one."

Little Irimi Dragon smiled and in his excitement, he flew up and through the trees laughing and singing happy tunes. "Dear Anita," he began as he flew back to her, "I came here today to tell you how much I love you. Every time I saw you, you always made me happy with the gentleness and kindness you showed."

Dear Anita looked with the tearing eyes of a loving parent to Little Irimi Nage and said, "You have given me great happiness with your kind words. You have also given me great happiness with the gentleness and kindness that you showed to protect the wind from harm. You are the love of Aikido. I love you too, little one."

With my dear Anita's love in his heart, Little Irimi Nage knew his visit was complete. He kissed her lightly on the side of her cheek and then headed into the sky, singing a little song to her. "Dear Anita, I love you. You make me happy when I see you. Thank you for your kindness and love. Dragon Queen Ryu, I love you."

Dear Anita woke up the next morning filled with an abundance of gentleness, kindness, and happiness that could only be found through the love of an innocent baby dragon named Little Irimi Nage. How very proud she was of Little Irimi Nage for his chivalry toward the universe. He gallantly had entrusted her with his love and courage. My dear Anita knew that he was an angel from the universe meant to open her heart further into the spirituality of Aikido. She kept his love and courage endearingly in her heart and dojo.

Training, training, and more training continued in the dojo with my dear Anita aka Ana Sensei. The spirit of Little Irimi Nage was always near. Being Ana Sensei during this time gave her great joy to be of service to the students and to see their transformation take place in the dojo. She loved to see the change in their state of mind and watch their cheeks grow red as they trained and learned with lots of energy. Fun, happiness, and an upbeat feeling of freedom grew stronger with every deshi's heartbeat found in her classes. It did her heart great to know they were learning the fine art of Aikido protection.

Aikido protection and spirituality were soon to embrace dear Anita's treehouse dojo in the sky. One morning, after much non-stop rain the skies began to partially clear as the sun tried to filter through upon the dojo. Classes and breakfast were over, and dear Anita was in her home looking at the bayou. She had noticed it had risen over the course of the past couple of days due to all the rain. The sun, though it was attempting to shine, was being covered once more by darkening rain clouds. Hard rains with thick, heavy drops of water started pounding once more. Within two hours, the bayou was rising out of its banks and flowing into the grounds. Logs, ducks, and snakes were floating atop the water. The bayou water was overflowing into the pool. Anita, alone in the house, became the soul warrior to keep the dojo from becoming a watercraft. Quickly Anita put on black rubber boots and a rain slicker and proceeded to and fro across the red bridge emptying out the dojo of O'Sensei's picture, artwork, Izunome's figurine, bokkens, staffs, and shinais. Back and forth she went across the red spiraling bridge from the dojo to her home. Lastly, she opened all the windows and left the door ajar to the dojo to prevent pressure from building up inside. Dear Anita safely stored all the items within the dojo inside of her home.

With a calm heart, dear Anita lit eleven (a spiritual, angelic number that holds the connection to one's guardian angels and brings happiness and joy) candles throughout her home and said prayers to all the deities that surround her life that nothing would happen to the dojo. After finishing her prayers she filled her heart with more love and gratitude to all she had prayed and peacefully accepted the wisdom of the universe to let be what was meant to be. Let it be.

The rain kept coming in strong sheets of thick, heavy rain as the wind blew in a cross angle direction toward the dojo. The bayou waters continued to rise with steadfast determination. Dear Anita could no longer see the pool, and only the tops of her plants were visible. A loving thought of Abuela Ana came into her mind. She saw Abuela Ana as the revolutionist she once was. She was dressed in pants, a shirt, and boots, and her face held an intense look of strong-mindedness. She was preparing to take amicable action toward those who were causing unnecessary discord and harm. Lovingly she said to dear Anita, "Your prayers are very powerful, my dear. You have the strength of a revolutionist's conviction of truth and fairness to all, the compassion of a warrior, and the love of an angel. Rest tonight, my dear, with beautiful thoughts of the dojo. The universe will abide accordingly. I am forever near you with love."

Dear Anita's thoughts and heart were shining, as if they were the sun, with joy and peace. She took one last look at the treehouse dojo now blurry with the darkened sky and relentless rain. She saw what appeared to be murky water reaching the dojo's door. In her gentlest of thoughts, she embraced the dojo in her hands and kissed it kindly with love and respect as one of her tears protectively fell upon its roof. Listening to Abuela Ana's advice, dear Anita went to sleep and dreamed only beautiful thoughts of the treehouse dojo being surrounded by a calm, cloudless, light blue and soft, sunny sky. O'Sensei would be proud!

My dear Anita woke up very early the next morning feeling rested and full of energy. She could see from her bedroom window that the sky was still dark, but she could not hear rain or the sound of rising water. She literally jumped out of the bed, grabbed her kimono, and tied it as she ran full force toward the dojo. At first, dear Anita could not tell if the dojo was there or not due to the dark sky. She looked to no avail and saw nothing. Then slowly, ever so slowly, the moon peered from the dark clouds and cast its reflection on the receding waters across the grounds. Within the reflection, she could see the rippling outline of a roof, and then a small building with open windows and a door slightly ajar (as if welcoming her in). The treehouse dojo was there! Exuberance filled Anita's heart and body. She zoomed up the red spiral bridge to the door as the moon shined bright light upon her path and the dojo. Suddenly, she stopped solid in her tracks, for she saw two intrusions caused by the bayou's murky waters. First, there was a small water moccasin snake slithering near Anita's feet. In a kind and no-nonsense tone of voice, dear Anita told the snake he did not belong there and for him to return immediately to his home in the bayou. Without question, the snake complied.

Second, dear Anita saw water lines on the statues outside the dojo. Then she saw water lines approximately eighteen inches up the dojo. The wood of the dojo door was wet. Swiftly and with care, she opened further the ajarred dojo door and stepped inside. The floor was dry! She took three more steps and turned on the light. All of the dojo was dry! The floor was dry. The walls were dry. The open windows on the inside were dry. As well as the inside of the dojo door. Without a moment's thought, dear Anita ran back into her house and returned with O'Sensei's photo and placed back it on the wall. She kneeled and bowed before him in gratitude and love. It gave dear Anita great joy to have O'Sensei's photo safely where it belonged. The spirit of Aikido was in full loving force!

As dear Anita left the dojo that morning, she never questioned the water lines on the outside of the dojo and the dryness within its space. Within her heart eleven candles were victoriously illuminating the heavenly glow of love, the universe, Abuela Ana, Izunome, the spirituality of Aikido and all the loved ones that morning, noon, and night always remain graciously and lovingly as safeguards by her side. Love was always all around my dear Anita whether it be yesterday, today, or tomorrow!

Expanding changes were taking place in dear Anita's life away from the dojo. The universe once more was bringing to her blessings in disguise. She full heartedly accepted all that was coming into her life's path. Once, in a dream, I told my dear Anita that adapting is one of the keys to a harmonious life. She smiled gently, in her sleep, when she heard my words. Please, keep in mind, adapting is not a passive way of accepting that which is around. No, it is more of a conscious way of going in unison with change and making the change become you. In adapting lies one's truth to that which is meant to be and living it to the fullest without comparison to what was or what if. One of these disguised blessings was for Anita to move to a new home.

Dear Anita reached out to three Realtors and explained she needed a house large enough to hold celebrations with her family and friends and that it must have sizeable grounds to build a dojo. All three Realtors told her that they could not help her due to the various zoning laws and deed restrictions in Houston. They went further to say that she was asking for the impossible. My dear Anita kindly thanked them all, but she paid no mind to their answers. You never tell a dragon no nor do you tell them something is impossible. Those two words never have nor will they ever exist for a dragon.

Later that evening, while in contemplation regarding her move, a single word came to her—Hawthorne. Now, dear Anita was familiar with the Hawthorn plant and the author Nathaniel Hawthorne, but she was not sure how it applied to her having a new home. Nonetheless, she acknowledged and thanked the word. The next morning, dear Anita decided to get in her car and drive around the city to look at the various homes. She had always been fond of the Montrose area in Houston, so she headed in that direction. While driving down Montrose Boulevard she saw a street named Yupon and remembered the Rothko Chapel (a place where many Houstonians of different spiritual beliefs go to pray). Instinctually, she took this as a sign and made a right turn onto the street. Almost immediately she came to the cross street of Hawthorne. "Hawthorne," dear Anita exclaimed to herself. "Hawthorne, are you serious?" she said out loud to the universe! She turned her head slightly to the left and saw at the corner of Yupon and Hawthorne a huge three-story home with nine beautiful and very old oak trees on an oversized corner lot for sale. Dear Anita called the number on the For Sale sign and discovered that the Realtor was the same one who had sold her her current home. The Realtor asked Anita to please wait and she would be there in a few minutes to show her the house.

Another thing you don't tell a dragon is to wait! My dear Anita was out of that car quicker than a flash of lightning! Although she could not go into the house, she was able to walk the grounds. Beauty was everywhere. My dear Anita was falling in love by the milliseconds. As she followed the nine oak trees, she found her way to a pool. Quickly, she thought, *I don't need a pool. I need a dojo. I will build the dojo over the pool.* Dear Anita continued to explore the grounds and create the possibility of what was to be.

When the Realtor arrived both she and dear Anita went inside the house. Only to dear Anita, it was not a house. It was a loving home filled with spirituality! The owner of the home, who was also the builder, was present and assisted in showing dear Anita the home. The owner and Anita created a wonderful rapport almost immediately. She being Cuban and he being Colombian, they had a great deal of thoughts and ideas in common. They began to discuss the layout of the home and negotiations in Spanish. He told Anita that his son, who was an architect, had designed the home for him. The home was just as huge and breathtaking on the inside as it was on the outside. Lots of ceiling-to-floor windows letting in all of the universe's light! The home had been designed in perfect Feng Shui! My dear Anita could feel the love, tenderness, and great attention to detail that had been given to this home. Synchrodestiny was welcoming my dear Anita to be the new dweller of the home!

Anita explained to the builder of her plans to build a dojo for the Shobu Aikido Houston School. She mentioned she was thinking of placing the dojo over the pool. The owner informed her that yes it was possible to do as the grounds were very large and that there were no zoning laws in Montrose. My dear Anita's heart was singing with joy! Within moments, dear Anita was manifesting both the home and dojo to be in her future. With equal parts of earnestness and laughter, Anita, in Spanish, said to the owner, "My new home is beautiful, isn't it?" And with that straightforward statement, the negotiations began and the home became my dear Anita's!

Once my dear Anita moved into the Hawthorne house, she began the designs for the new dojo. Dear Anita was blessed once more with synchrodestiny and lots of help from amazing individuals who made the building of the school remarkable. The original chosen architect proved to be too expensive, so he recommended one of his friends to build the dojo for less. Anita never forgot his kindness. All the right people came together at the right time. The designing of the dojo and all the many permits from the city (for building and commercial operations) all fell swiftly and smoothly in place. My dear Anita's gratitude is forever shining in her heart for all who made the dojo come to life. The second dojo was much larger and on the ground! She had the pool emptied of water and began the foundation for the dojo. She thought it was both humorous and most appropriate to have the dojo over the pool because Aikido is a water martial art. Water flows in the direction of that which is least resistant. Although water takes the least resistant route, that does not mean that it is weak. Water is love! Water is peace! Water is consciousness in its purest form! Water when in one with nature follows the course of the universe. Look how the oceans hold such wonderful and beautiful sea life. Think of the ocean waves as they roll onto the shores of the beach and then gently flow back to reunite with the sea. Hear the rains as they fall and give nourishment in rejuvenating and creating new life around the planet. And yes, water sometimes has the force to take away or eliminate when it becomes out of alignment with nature and the universe, but this is usually caused by other forces that have been unnaturally put upon its path. Are not the principles the same in Aikido? When a nage meets with the uke, does the nage not make their movements toward a peaceful resolution using love and compassion to keep the uke from harm? Sometimes, though, an unknown opponent may have such force in an ill-will intent that a peaceful resolution cannot be found. Harm may have to be regrettably inflicted as the last resort. When harm is done to one, it is done to the other. Everything must go full circle to have a resolution. The natural flow of water upon the earth is to sustain the harmony of life in the same manner as Aikido's movements are to bring into being peaceful, compassionate resolutions with all lives.

My dear Anita was very excited about the new dojo. She had it perfect in every way. The deshis had to walk through her gardens to get to the dojo, which was located in the northeast section of the grounds. Northeast in Feng Shui is the area of knowledge! The Japanese-style gardens, whose walkway had been designed slowly and peacefully with love by a war veteran who got his inspirations from his Japanese wife, had a mixture of different blooming plants that were visited daily by butterflies and dragonflies. As deshis continued to walk, they would pass a wonderful little wooden bridge near a flowing fountain that naturally sang sweet, calming songs of nature. As they followed the slightly twisting path, they would pass a beautiful pond whose trickling waters danced in rhythm with the movements of the wind's gentle breezes. All the while in the background, eleven large, magnificent metal chimes of all different sizes would sound their harmonious tones of a warrior's preparedness to learn and laugh in courage as they take on the forms of uke and nage in the dojo.

Like the first dojo, when the deshis entered through the wooden doors they were greeted with love and blessings by Izunome. Light from all the oversized windows filled the dojo with brightness and positive, peaceful energies of Takemusu Aiki (Enlightened Aikido). The floors were a hidden marvel within themselves. Another blessing for dear Anita is that a longtime student of Saotome Sensei's came to Houston to install the floors. On the surface were the handmade green tatami mats (which are filled with layers of soft straw and a foam center). Below the tatami mats was carpeting, then quarter-inch gymnastic mats, then two layers of plywood, and at the very bottom four-inch rubber squares placed sixteen inches apart. The walls were lined with racks of Aikido practice weapons to include bookens (wooden practice swords), jos (short staffs), tantos (wooden practice knives), and shinais (split bamboo practice swords). The shomen held the picture of O'Sensei and the ceiling-to-floor Ai Ki Do calligraphy. Two wooden shelves on opposite sides of the calligraphy held a small shrine (with fresh flowers) and Izunome (with her 108 prayer beads). Near the shomen were two additional Japanese calligraphies that read Aikido and Shobu. These were beloved gifts given to my dear Anita by Saotome Sensei.

Dear Anita, with the extraordinary help from one of her deshis, created a website for Shobu Aikido Houston (www.ShobuAikidoHouston. com) to inform future deshis of the Aikido school, its evening class schedule, and that the school would be opening in a month, welcoming them to become members. A quick note to make is that the deshis who created the website had never created a website before and is now a great and very successful website developer. Synchrodestiny in motion once more! Anita, from having written them during the time of the first dojo, had all the training lesson plans needed in order to teach. In her always enthusiastic manner, my dear Anita was visiting the dojo every day prior to opening to review and refine the techniques of her lesson plans. She wanted the future deshis to have the very best in their practice and training. Dear Anita wanted them to have within them not only confidence and courage but the ever-growing trust of the universe to guide them to the appropriate technique needed for any situation. My dear Anita also remembered the distinguished words

Saotome Sensei had gifted her with when she joined the ASU. He graciously shared with her that people do not follow your techniques; they follow your heart. He told dear Anita that she had a heart filled with love, and this was the way to teach Aikido. Saotome Sensei had also told dear Anita that he envisioned a place of Aikitopia where there is only a harmonious world that encompasses compassionate warriors in an environment of Aikido's purest love. He honored dear Anita by saying she was a reflection of this beautiful environment. My dear Anita always kept Saotome Sensei's gifted words in her heart and shared them generously with her deshis by establishing a safe dojo haven created with the joy, love, jokes, and laughter needed for them to enfold the spirit of Aikido's honor and love on their evolving pathway as compassionate warriors.

My dear Anita, as you know, has always been surrounded by love and protection, and with the second dojo came another guardian of protection. It was one of her new deshis who had joined the school during the opening year. He silently, at first, and with the strength of will and instincts of a wise wolf watched over the dojo. He always was thinking ahead, studying, and doing research on the proper things that needed to be done to ensure that everything was of impeccable standards and the way it should be. He would double-check to make sure that there was plenty of soap and all essentials needed in the locker rooms and wash areas. He repaired the walls with metal mesh to enforce them with strength against the occasional too-long rolls that would cause feet to hit hard against them. He had great respect for dear Anita, his Ana Sensei. He welcomed her in his heart and protective nature. When the time was right, he would advise dear Anita of things that may be needed for the dojo. He helped to ensure the grounds around the dojo were in perfect order and all flowed smoothly around and within the dojo. He created a beautiful metal sculpture of a large, blue, open circle where inside resided a yellow triangle encasing a red square. The sculpture symbolized the earth, fire, and water elements that intertwine the centered ground presence, heart energies, and spiral movements of Aikido. Most recently he brought to being two dragon statues in the west and east parts of the grounds. My dear Anita was truly blessed, once more in life, to have her dojo guardian! She gratefully refers to him as the Wolf Guardian!

Spirituality was flowing more rapidly and freely around my dear Anita. The words by and inner journeys learned from Deepak Chopra and Jean Houston were moving forward at full speed ahead for dear Anita. Spirituality and Aikido were taking on new spheres of strengths for Anita through her discoveries of self in regard to the link between spirituality and science of cosmic consciousness. The reliving of her three near-death experiences gave dear Anita loving inspiration that in the domains of death there is no end, only new beginnings to one's life force. The potentialities she found in her archetypes of Izunome and Dragon were infinite. The times she visited the Dragon Counsel to learn of being Dragon Queen Ryu and the beauty that rested in her healing hands of a dragon gave her great joy and belief in being of service to both the dragons and humankind. The wondrous times my dear Anita and I spent alone together talking about the realms of dragons and how magnificent and loving we are with ourselves and all that is of the universe gave her additional inner strengths to express spirituality in the dojo. My dear Anita knew that all these new journeys and empowering dragon energies of exuberant confidence also created limitless freedoms for herself and her deshis.

As dear Anita's thoughts expanded into her higher consciousness, she knew she must remove all manmade complexities with the simplicities of a dragon's determination, Izunome's love, and Dragon Queen Ryu's healing to bring forth even more spirituality within the dojo. From her mind's eye, she saw the interior of the dojo with her deshis inside training peacefully with one another. She saw the picture of O'Sensei watching them in silence with pride. Dear Anita saw Izunome floating in a beautiful white flowing gown as she circled the room freely, sending the beauty of her love throughout the dojo. Saotome Sensei's book *Aikido and the Harmony of Nature* was open to page eighteen, where his calligraphy for the term Kannagara No Michi (the Way of God) was showing. Saotome Sensei suddenly entered dear Anita's heart with his words. "Very courageous to speak spirituality. Bring to heart." My dear Anita's heart and soul wept tears of happiness for the beauty that she had just been shown. The simplicities of spirituality were being guided with love into the dojo.

Although they still remained exact in her mind and flowed effortlessly in her teachings with the deshis, dear Anita gradually released the structure of the lesson plans she had created for the first dojo. She began to meditate before every class and within her meditation, the techniques and energies to be taught would be revealed to her from the heart of the universe. Being Sensei was taking on a wider path of fun, relaxation, and let it be. It was a wonderful feeling to be of service to her deshis and see their transformation in an upbeat manner of joy and happiness. By releasing emphasis on the paper lesson plans and empowering the loving spiritedness of meditation, more awareness of Aikido's courage and peaceful compassion was coming into the dojo. Freedom from the ego was to become a natural vibration of love moving forward.

New energies were spreading quickly throughout my dear Anita's body, mind, and spirit. In these energies, she kept hearing the phrase "the kindness of the heart reigns!" Dear Anita's state of mind was shifting her belief of "Expect Nothing and Be Ready for Everything" to encompass the belief of "Expect Nothing and Be Grateful for Everything." Dear Anita was connecting to an inner peace that she was experiencing in her daily meditation and knew that now was the time to introduce the techniques to such inner peace to her classes. She began holding meditation sessions before the start of classes so that deshis may relax and have a calm state of mind while training in Aikido. The mindfulness of meditation gave freshness and freedom to the body's fluid, thus releasing all blockage and stagnation. Meditational training of spirit would create for the deshis a place of "just being" as they began to train on the mats with their bodies. My dear Anita brought to life the saying "Advance Aikido Training Is Meditation in Motion." Dear Anita knew that spirit and body must be as one in awareness to combat all obstacles that may be found in Aikido training and daily life. As meditation was happening, dear Anita would play heart sutras to include Izunome chants to awaken the heart and summon strengths of love. Peace and harmony filled the dojo!

The spirituality of music continued into the warm-ups that followed the meditation. My dear Anita knew that music and laughter were sounds of the Gods! She remembered that Confucius was a great lover of music and that he believed music transformed the consciousness to increase its capacity and compassion. Confucius believed that music should be played at all times, for it would develop a joyous heart and shift society into a better being. Much-beloved O'Sensei in his teachings spoke frequently of Kotodama (the spiritual sounds of Aikido) and how they released the spiritual strengths found in Aikido. It was Saotome Sensei who gave dear Anita the vision to have music within the dojo. She had remembered the first technique that he had related to music, specifically the waltz was Ikkyo. Saotome Sensei would emphasize how the rhythms found in a waltz can be at one with the movements of Aikido and how harmoniously they would affect the soul and flow deep into the center of one's body. Dear Anita understood his words. In her mind, she could feel a Chopin waltz playing as she moved in body, mind, and spirit on the mat. She held this feeling always!

Once at one of Saotome Sensei's seminars being held in Philadelphia, dear Anita decided to put music in the warm-up prior to keiko (training on the mat). She had discussed bringing the music into the seminar with one of the Aikido master swordsmen named David. He was in agreement that this would be fine and an excellent learning technique. Dear Anita proceeded to play the classical music, and she, David, and the other attendees moved in perfect rhythm to Aikido and Mozart. Saotome Sensei entered the room. He had not heard dear Anita's introduction that the music was intended only as a prelude to the Aikido training in order to release stiffness of the joints and mind. Needless to say, Saotome Sensei was not amused. He went directly to Anita and David. To Anita, he said, "Dojo martial arts. No dancing. You forget purpose. To face death. To be under the live blade." Saotome Sensei was not done with dear Anita, yet. He pulled out his live sword before dear Anita's face and said, "No dancing! You focus. Always. You play you die. Life or death." As a deshi, dear Anita remained in total respect to her Sensei and listened with a full heart to what he said and did. As she saw the gleaming metal sword moving before her eyes she thought to herself with sincerity and slight humor, *This is a good day to die if I must!* Then with the utmost of calm, Saotome Sensei ended his words, retreated his live sword, turned, and proceeded to begin the seminar. My dear Anita watched her Sensei in awe as he moved away. She smiled with benevolence as she placed herself in seiza. Saotome Sensei immediately called on David to attack him as fast as he could. As David swiftly moved toward him, Saotome Sensei with the lightest touch had him spinning high in the air. High up he rose, as if weightless, and with the pull of gravity back to the mat he landed with a resounding thud. Saotome Sensei simply smiled. Not with hostility or meanness, but with humor and love. His techniques were powerful and effective in teaching his ukes of his profound knowledge of peace and compassion for one's attacker. Within a few minutes, Saotome Sensei called upon dear Anita to demonstrate with him another Aikido technique. Each with their hearts of kindness moved as one energy in unison before the attendees. As the technique concluded with perfect resolution, dear Anita surmised that she was eternally grateful for having not died that day, because there was so much more to learn from and to be of service to her beloved Sensei. As irony would have it they would dance together later that evening to the loud music playing over the disco speakers. There was no talk of life or death during this dance. Only the compassionate feelings of life, love, and laughter that are found through respect for one another and the spirit of Aikido!

My dear Anita had been playing classical music previous to the seminar during the pre-keiko warm-ups within her own classes. It was the positive results she observed that inspired her to present them to Saotome Sensei. With her deshis, she could see and feel how the rhythm of the music would flow smoothly into the deshis's bodies, heart center, and hara, allowing harmony to move freely throughout their given movements. The harmony would remain flowing within them as they moved on with keiko with each other, allowing them to have increased concentration, more freedom in movement release of mind, and a spiritual connection between hara, head, and heart. The same would hold true when she began to introduce the rhythmic movements of the cha-cha-cha in the warm-ups. Harmony, smiles, laughter, and love filled the body, mind, soul, and dojo!

With music coming into full energy, so began the spiritual healing powers of Dragon Queen Ryu. One afternoon, after the warm-ups were completed, my dear Anita, as she always did, began the class bowing and giving great gratitude to O'Sensei. Suddenly, she began to feel a strong feeling of knowing. The feeling grew stronger and surrounded her with love. Dear Anita could feel O'Sensei's presence of Ryu. The feeling was telling her that it was time to acknowledge the responsibility of Ryu. The dragons needed to be brought into reality and no longer kept in the shadow. Entering her spirit was the remembrance of the days spent at the Dragon Council and how she had been told of the Dragon Realm and her healing hands of the Dragon Queen Ryu. Tears of joy ran down her cheeks, for at the same moment she felt Izunome's love filling her heart. My dear Anita remembered, too, her promise to Izunome that she would always help others and would never allow her own ego to take credit. The energy of love was at its fullest within her body, mind, and spirit, for she was embraced by the love of O'Sensei, Izunome, and Dragons. The love energies flowed all over her body, allowing the new healing energy of Dragon Queen Ryu to come to life. As my dear Anita turned and bowed into her class of deshis, she sent natural and infinite healing love to them. And lovingly, for I will never forget, she said to me in thought, "My dear Aiki Dragon, I am graciously overfilled with gratitude and love for you and all the dragons. My heart is growing stronger and stronger with this love, and I promise you I will now begin to set you and all the dragons free into the world of mankind." I had never felt words of beauty and truth resonate throughout my body and heart with such enthusiasm as those that my dear Anita had just spoken. Through her genuine enthusiasm, my dear Anita had just given me the most beautiful gift of love that could be given to me. For if my dear Anita said something, it became so. I knew within my heart that we dragons would become once more a part of the world of mankind where we could live amongst them with honor in love and harmony.

Beginning with this class and in all subsequent classes, my dear Anita became forever in sync with the extra fluidity and flexibility that we dragons have within ourselves, which allow us to have quick movements, thoughts, and wits. Such fluidity and flexibility allow for more calmness of mind and relaxation of body to flow in the same way an autumn leaf connects with the breeze and gently yet dynamically spirals up into the sky and then falls naturally to the ground. Within the spiral turns of the leaf, energies of regeneration are created, for it will once again be part of the earth, giving its energy to that which it touches. For us dragons, the spiral energies become those of healing. My dear Anita, through her transformation as Dragon Queen Ryu, was able to release her healing energies through her spirals with her deshis. As she gently took the lightest touch upon her deshi's hand, she would momentarily capture their energy of intent and lovingly move it forward as together they spiraled upward like two kindhearted dragons in flight. All the while her great healing energies of love were being released from her hara into the warmth of the Dragon Queen Ryu's hands and fingers, where they flowed majestically from her fingertips in great abundance to her deshi's heart. Then, as they spiraled downward to the ground, the energy of intent lost its need to be. The deshi's spirit having been embraced with the healing energy became victorious and showed its appreciation through joy, laughter, and smiles! The Dragon Realm of Health and Happiness had come to life! As Dragon Queen Ryu, my dear Anita knew that happiness gives rise to healthiness!

My dear Anita would show them how they could feel the healing energy within their own hands by simply asking them to bring their hands slowly together. As their hands came closer and closer, they could feel the energy surging between their hands and within their fingers. Also, at the end of every class, she would ask for two ukes to come forward. She would ask them to stand in front of her in a row one behind the other. The front deshi would extend their hand, in a fist, as if their intent was to thrust a blow to her chest. With divine love and compassion, my dear Anita (aka Dragon Queen Ryu) would open her heart as she stood self-grounded in a confidence stance of kamae and look beyond the face of the back uke (to direct their intent to a more harmonious direction), and release her healing energy of love from her hara, to and through her benevolent heart, down her arms and to her hands, setting it free from her fingertips. Once her fingertips lightly, ever so lightly, touched the front uke's fist of intent, both ukes would become powerless and would be jolted back due to the transfer of the Dragon Queen Ryu's healing energies of love to their body, mind, and spirit. Once more joy, laughter, and smiles would abound! Amazement and admiration radiated throughout the dojo! Once a uke has been touched by the Dragon Queen Ryu's healing energy of love, it remains with them always! They, too, have the same healing power to use with other ukes (of the class or from elsewhere). Healing through the heart's energy of love was forever in progress!

There was also another form of spirituality that dear Anita brought into the dojo that she had learned from Saotome Sensei's esteemed heart of love and compassion. This was the silent spirituality of not embarrassing or humiliating a deshi. Nor would he allow any harm to come to his deshis. He gave them strength in his friendly phrase of "If I can do it, you can do it." My dear Anita would always compliment the well-performed techniques with full-spirited exaltation and acknowledge the not-so-well-performed techniques with love and kind guidance toward refinement. In Aikido, as in the universe, there is no right or wrong. Only the grace of love and kindness moving forward in unification to create peace, harmony, and oneness with all who dwell within its sphere.

My dear Anita, like the spiral moves in Aikido, was always present, whether it was in person, in her thoughts, or in her dreams. Her world was past, present, and future all in one. Spirituality remained by Anita's side wherever she was present. Even in her dreams. My dear Anita began to have a recurring snake dream. In her dream she was in a room filled with many people, and a large snake would enter. She would warn the people of the snake and inform them that they needed to get out of the room. Nobody, except for Anita, would leave the room. Dear Anita mentioned this dream to Dr. Houston, and she told dear Anita that she needed to practice Kundalini. "Anita," Dr. Houston began, "Kundalini is like a snake that is coiled at the first chakra at the base of your spine and longing to be released. Your spiritual energy, like the snake in your dream, has been awakened and is ready to partake in a new journey. The snake is not a foe but a friend. Through Kundalini your spiritual energy will travel through all your chakras until it reaches the chakra of the crown of your head, where it enlightens you with higher consciousness."

My dear Anita was liking what she was hearing, and her enthusiasm was going at warp speed! She thanked Dr. Houston and began to learn all she could about Kundalini. She began by gathering all the books she could find. She read each book, highlighting the words and phrases she wanted to remember or grasp a better understanding of. Next to her was her dictionary ready for vocabulary clarity! She was fascinated by it all! After finishing and noting all her Kundalini books, dear Anita decided it was time to practice Kundalini in person with others. As synchrodestiny would have it, there was an ashram, where Kundalini was practiced and taught, four blocks from her home. It had been started by the spiritual leader Yogi Bahjan. He came to the United States the same year as Saotome Sensei (synchrodestiny, again). She took two classes and decided she wanted to learn even more. My dear Anita's motto of "what better way to learn than to teach" came to life once more. She decided to become certified as an international Kundalini teacher (which was new. No individuals had been certified previously through the ashram before). The training was for nine long weekends (Thursday through Sunday from 4:30 a.m. to 6:00 p.m. and sometimes until 8:00 p.m.). After she had signed up for the certification classes, Anita kidded with herself that she didn't read the fine print! She didn't truly realize the extent of the hours, days, weeks that this training would entail. Nonetheless, though, as you know, once my dear Anita begins something, she always sees it through to the end!

Kundalini tugged at my dear Anita's heart because she had knowledge that O'Sensei (Morihei Ueshiba) practiced many of the techniques and disciplines found in Kundalini during his lifetime. In respect and love for O'Sensei, dear Anita wanted to feel what he had felt. After becoming certified dear Anita decided it was time to complete the 1,000-day Kundalini sadhana (a spiritual daily practice where meditating and chanting give power and release of one's higher consciousness while the ego remains quiet and still). Although Kundalini was never what my dear Anita would refer to as a burden, it was very detailed and authoritative of discipline. Now, for dear Anita, detail and discipline are delightful! So she had no difficulties whatsoever!

My dear Anita would wake up at 3:30 a.m. every morning for 1,000 days. She would take a cold shower, brush her teeth (including the cleaning of her tongue all the way to the back), brush her hair, and oil her body. After this, she would dress all in white cotton (including a white wrap to cover her hair, beginning at the hairline at the ears, so all the power found within her hair would remain). She would then light candles and sit in seiza and hold her posture while she moved in various yoga positions; she meditated and chanted several mantras while engaging in three different types of breath (her favorite was the breath of fire with its rapid, deep inhalation and exhalations that create good health and strength)! Dear Anita's Kundalini sadhana would last approximately two and a half hours each morning. Now, the 1,000 days mean a 1,000 *consistent* days. No days can be missed. If a day is missed you have to begin all over (even if you are on day 999)! Proudly I tell you, my dear Anita did not miss a single day. Of course, to not miss a single day meant that sometimes when Anita was away from home, she did her Kundalini wherever she could, including in friends' closets and taxi cabs! My dear Anita and I laugh with each other when we remember a New York taxi driver's face as she was doing her Kundalini. It was a face of compassion, yet it still had the look of "Okay, lady, do whatever you need to do. It's cool!" It did not faze him in the least on the outside. On the inside, though, I believe it did faze him with an abundance of my dear Anita's pure love!

After 1,000 days of Kundalini, my dear Anita had mixed emotions. In her playful and humorous mind, she told herself, *I'll never do that again!* In her mind and heart of love, she was very grateful for the 1,000 days, for they brought forth new feelings of healing love and compassion. She experienced angelic consciousness within her body from the sound currents she produced from her daily chanting. These tied in with her gift of being a frequency orchestrator that she joyously created with her students in the dojo, though they did not know it. Her loving thoughts for those who came into her world would manifest into their world and change their own frequencies into love and peace. My dear Anita had universal proof of this from observing her deshis. As some of her deshis entered the dojo, she could see burdened looks filled with the demands of their day. In silence, she always sent them love, beauty, and well-being. On the mat, she instilled a harmonious environment of laughter and love. She sent her healing energies of love with every touch that she bestowed upon them. The music in the dojo was of Izunome's love and the universal rhythm of Aikido's victorious movements. At the end of class, she could see how all her students had transformed into Aikidokas of happiness and love. She could feel their excitement for having been in the moment of Aikido's peaceful and harmonious spirit. Just as a classical pianist brings to life keys of the piano to create emotions for their audience, so does my dear Anita as a frequency orchestrator bring to life healing energies of love to create invincibility for her deshis. The invincibility would include the inner self courage, confidence, and calmness needed in the face of fear and danger (which may be that which presents itself to one whether in the form of a known or unknown uke or situations in one's daily life). Remember one may have fear and courage at the same time (Yin and

Yang), but with courage, one will be victorious in facing the realities of death before them and gaining the strengths to live each day as though it may be their last (for one day you will be right). Love, peace, and harmony live in courage!

As I am Aiki Dragon, I want to tell you of a beautiful story that my dear Anita told me of herself and Saotome Sensei. She was in one of his seminars in seiza, and Saotome Sensei called up the seven largest men in the room. My dear Anita thought to herself how in wonderment she was with him at that moment because he purposely was setting himself in a position of non-proportionate odds against seven large men who would attempt to cause harm. My dear Anita never had doubts, but she did have concerns of those almost seven-foot men against one five-foot-two man. Then Saotome Sensei pointed to her. She turned around, thinking he meant someone else. He did not. "No, no, no. You. You come here. You do it," he said. You see, when your Sensei asks you to come before the class, it is an honor that they bestow upon you. With no ego, my dear Anita's heart was beating with love and esteem for Saotome Sensei and his kindness. She wanted to do what he asked not for herself, but for him. With one touch of the energy from her finger, dear Anita was able to send her healing energy of love through all seven men, causing them to fall down like pins in a bowling alley! Both she and Saotome Sensei spontaneously began jumping up and down. In laughter and smiles, he said to her, "You did it. You did it!" This was a moment that my dear Anita has always cherished!

The beauty, love, and compassion of my dear Anita are perpetual. She did that technique for Saotome Sensei and not for herself. This is how my dear Anita has been all of her life. She has always wanted to be of service to others. Her father, Mr. Arango, used to call her, with love in his heart, a little Cuban Ambassador. As a child, she wanted to be a missionary to help the poor and indigent. Later as an attorney, she saved souls. As Dragon Queen Ryu she has always had the gift to walk into a room and uplift all those around. Through Aikido she joyously and gratefully gives her healing energies of love to her deshis. My dear Anita's honorable mission to be of service and share her heart of infinite love is forever constant and flourishes with all those (whether human, dragon, deity or nature) who enter upon her pathway of a compassionate warrior!

Epilogue

Forever Anita

My dear Anita jokes with me that as a little girl she had the mindset and guiding principles of the Lone Ranger. Which is very true. The ones that come to my mind immediately are 1) everyone has the power within themselves to make this a better world, 2) the belief in creator, country, and fellow man, 3) being prepared physically, mentally, and morally to fight when necessary for that which is right, 4) all men are created equal, and 5) all things change but truth, and truth alone lives forever. My dear Anita, aka my dear Kemosabe!

My dear Anita has always been a believer in all that surrounds her whether it be of the physical, spiritual, or imagination. She trusts through her courageous heart of love. Not too long ago she made a statement to me that once heard resonated from my ears to my heart (where it still lives). She stated, "Self-trust is self-confidence." Think about her words. If you trust in yourself with all your heart to do that which needs to be done, without questioning, having concerns about your comforts, or the elements of time and then do that which needs to be done, you will always have your own self at your side. You will have self-confidence because you are the one who makes it happen by always completing what you started. This is my dear Anita's secret energy, which has always been in her body, mind, and spirit. It is within her ki of enthusiasm. It has been the powerful, embracing, loving force that has led her down her many paths of being a peaceful, compassionate warrior in all that she accomplishes. And all she will continue to accomplish even more in her life learnings, spirituality, writings, and Aikido. There are many new adventures and possibilities that have and will be presented to my dear Anita. Her trust in them all will make her victorious! My dear enthusiastic and victorious Anita!

In these writings you have been introduced to dragons which fills my heart with endless joy. My love for my dear Anita is like that of the universe's grandeur. There is no beginning and no end of my love and exaltation for her. At last, through her, dragons have been brought back into your realm of thoughts. If you ever feel a light weight on your shoulders, most likely it will be one of us giving you love and a little guidance. Every time you think of a dragon, please know that we are near you. Soon, my friends, you will be seeing us in a stronger, newer light. You will see us coming forward little by little in your life. You may be walking through your own life's path and see one of us in the form of artwork, jewelry, decoration, a dragonfly or perhaps in a children's book (or many) about Dragons!

Aiki Dragon!

Lightning Source UK Ltd.
Milton Keynes UK
UKHW020153120122
396998UK00009B/375/J